# Learning AngularJS for .NET Developers

Build single-page web applications using frameworks
that help you work efficiently and deliver great results

**Alex Pop**

[PACKT] open source*
PUBLISHING   community experience distilled

BIRMINGHAM - MUMBAI

# Learning AngularJS for .NET Developers

Copyright © 2014 Packt Publishing

First published: July 2014

Production reference: 1180714

Published by Packt Publishing Ltd.
Livery Place
35 Livery Street
Birmingham B3 2PB, UK.

ISBN 978-1-78398-660-6

www.packtpub.com

Cover image by Rajnish Jha (rajnishlalitjha@gmail.com)

# Credits

**Author**
Alex Pop

**Reviewers**
Andrew C Cunliffe
Anton Kropp
Pascal Precht

**Commissioning Editor**
Usha Iyer

**Acquisition Editor**
Richard Brookes-Bland

**Content Development Editor**
Arvind Koul

**Technical Editor**
Sebastian Michael Rodrigues

**Copy Editors**
Insiya Morbiwala
Aditya Nair

**Project Coordinator**
Neha Bhatnagar

**Proofreaders**
Maria Gould
Ameesha Green

**Indexers**
Hemangini Bari
Tejal Soni

**Graphics**
Valentina D'silva

**Production Coordinator**
Conidon Miranda

**Cover Work**
Conidon Miranda

# About the Author

**Alex Pop** is a professional software developer with a university degree in Computer Engineering and 12 years of commercial experience building .NET applications. He has worked for ISVs, building enterprise resource planning applications, content management systems, and insurance and financial software products, and he is currently working in the higher education sector as a web application developer. His developer blog at `http://alexvpop.blogspot.co.uk` contains technical articles about .NET, JavaScript, and various software engineering topics.

I would like to salute the efforts of the open source developer community at large that made this book possible. I would like to thank my ever-so-understanding wife and daughter who patiently supported me in writing this book.

# About the Reviewers

**Andrew C Cunliffe** is a technical consultant; he focuses on projects that use open source technologies and process improvements for development teams of all sizes. He delivers integrated, end-to-end solutions through the use of continuous delivery techniques, with more than 15 years of experience writing software for corporate companies, ranging from company tools such as intranets to large bespoke solutions used by governments and banks. Andrew has worked with a large number of software languages, predominantly JavaScript (AngularJS and Node.js), Java, and PHP. He always ensures the highest levels of quality through test-driven techniques. In his limited free time, he contributes to projects on GitHub and reviews books for publications. Andrew is the owner of SYSEN Ltd, where he holds the position of Director; SYSEN offers professional services in the software development and support landscape. The company has delivered solutions for a number of businesses; for more information, see the website, www.sysen.co.uk.

> I would not have been able to do all of this without the ongoing support of my family and friends, and as such, I would like to thank them all, especially my wife and our three children.

**Anton Kropp** is an ex-Amazon engineer, who is now Senior Software Engineer at Practice Fusion, where he works on web-based electronic health records. He has extensive experience with F#, C#, AngularJS, TypeScript, realtime video, and OCR, and he also runs the blog `www.onoffswitch.net`. Anton is currently based in Seattle and spends his free time riding his bicycle and drinking local beer.

**Pascal Precht** is a frontend engineer and has over 7 years of professional experience in web development. He loves semantic markup, evolving technologies, and the open Web. Pascal is very active in the community and has contributed to many open source projects, such as AngularJS and AngularUI, to name a few. He is also the creator of the popular angular-translate module for the AngularJS framework. Pascal has also reviewed *ng-book, Ari Lerner, Fullstack. io,* which is one of the most-read books about AngularJS. When he's not busy preparing for the next workshop or conference talk, you might find him outside with his skateboard.

# www.PacktPub.com

## Support files, eBooks, discount offers and more

You might want to visit www.PacktPub.com for support files and downloads related to your book.

Did you know that Packt offers eBook versions of every book published, with PDF and ePub files available? You can upgrade to the eBook version at www.PacktPub.com and as a print book customer, you are entitled to a discount on the eBook copy. Get in touch with us at service@packtpub.com for more details.

At www.PacktPub.com, you can also read a collection of free technical articles, sign up for a range of free newsletters and receive exclusive discounts and offers on Packt books and eBooks.

http://PacktLib.PacktPub.com

Do you need instant solutions to your IT questions? PacktLib is Packt's online digital book library. Here, you can access, read and search across Packt's entire library of books.

## Why subscribe?

- Fully searchable across every book published by Packt
- Copy and paste, print and bookmark content
- On demand and accessible via web browser

## Free access for Packt account holders

If you have an account with Packt at www.PacktPub.com, you can use this to access PacktLib today and view nine entirely free books. Simply use your login credentials for immediate access.

# Table of Contents

# Preface

In the last couple of years, the web development landscape has changed dramatically following the mainstream adoption of smartphones and tablets. Mobile web traffic has increased substantially in 2013 alone, reaching almost a third of the total web traffic and the increase is expected to continue in the near future. Websites are now expected to work on a wide range of devices and form factors and they have to support an unprecedented diversity of browser clients. Web applications based on browser plugins such as Java, Adobe Flash, and Silverlight have become problematic as these plugins are not available or not supported on all devices.

Parallel with these changes, all major browser vendors have accelerated the work to define and implement web standards such as HTML5 and CSS3 and JavaScript standards such as ECMAScript 5.1 and the upcoming ECMAScript 6. Although not all these standards are final or complete, a succession of browser releases from all vendors have continuously improved standards support and the performance of client-side content and code. The wider development community also contributed to the standardization effort by providing various tools and libraries. These have extended web standards support for older browsers and unified different browser implementations of similar features under a common programming model.

A new web development ecosystem based on open standards, tools, and libraries emerged. It was used as a solid base to build modern web applications that embrace HTML, CSS, and JavaScript rather than abstracting them away. It also allowed for applications based on browser plugins to be gradually replaced by new versions based on HTML, CSS, and JavaScript. The focus on leveraging client-browser capabilities for rendering and manipulating content led to the adoption of a new type of application called a single-page application. It was made popular by the Google Mail and Google Maps web applications, which were very responsive, easy to use, and had a look and feel similar to desktop applications.

A single-page application typically has initial resources and content generated server side on the first application request, and for all subsequent requests, it will use client-side code to load any required resources and display content. A single-page application can also have one or more static pages that serve as physical entry points. Microsoft and Google made this type of application a first-class citizen in the software development kits for their operating systems in the form of Windows Store apps and Chrome apps. Cross-platform mobile development has also embraced HTML, CSS, and JavaScript in frameworks such as PhoneGap/Apache Cordova. Single-page applications have transitioned from consumer-focused applications to enterprise-focused applications in development models like the ones introduced by Microsoft with apps for Office and apps for SharePoint in Office 2013 and SharePoint 2013.

The building of modern web applications that include single-page applications involves the adoption of development approaches such as responsive web design (when the application adapts seamlessly to the browser-client resolution and orientation) and progressive enhancement (when the application provides different content based on the browser-client capabilities and the available network connection). A need for rapid prototyping, rich client features, and the reality of having to maintain large JavaScript code bases are other aspects that make the development process challenging and costly when compared with typical desktop application development.

The rise and mass adoption of jQuery and its plugin ecosystem after 2006 addressed the problem of rich client features. The increasingly complex JavaScript code bases remained a challenge that started to be addressed by the adoption of test frameworks, such as QUnit in 2008 and Jasmine in 2010, and new application frameworks, such as Backbone.js and Knockout.js in 2010. The application frameworks were implementing derivatives of a software design pattern common in server-side web application frameworks such as ASP.NET MVC: the Model-View-Controller (MVC) pattern. This pattern makes a clear distinction between components such as application data and business rules represented by the Model and the presentation of the application data in any shape or format represented by the View. The Controller component sits in the middle, passing data to or from the Model and updating the View or responding to View changes that are passed to the Model. This abstraction brings benefits like better code reuse (the same Model can be used by multiple Views), testability (the Controller can be tested in isolation from the View), and a more efficient development workflow (for example, while the developer works on a Controller, the designer can modify the View).

In the same timeframe, another JavaScript framework called AngularJS was being developed at Google. This framework was also based on the MVC pattern, and its strong points were that it could enhance and extend HTML by adding new elements and declarative behavior, and it could be tested from the start using modular, composable code units. With the 1.0 release in 2012, and since 2013, its popularity has grown more and more, with the high points being the 1.2 release in late 2013 and its first conference, called ng-conf, in January 2014.

Reflecting the popularity of single-page applications, Microsoft has started to provide support for this new application paradigm with Visual Studio 2012. With Visual Studio 2013, this support was enhanced, and a couple of recent Visual Studio extensions provide excellent support for AngularJS. Now is a great time to learn AngularJS if you are a .NET developer.

The main focus of this book is on how to rapidly prototype and build modern web applications with AngularJS in the context of .NET development tools and frameworks. The book assumes the reader has already built websites, web applications, or web services using Microsoft technologies such as ASP.NET, ASP. NET MVC, Silverlight, or WCF and knows the fundamentals of HTML5, CSS3, JavaScript, jQuery, and ASP.NET MVC.

# What this book covers

*Chapter 1, Introducing AngularJS*, teaches the reader how to manipulate HTML using AngularJS. The reader will also learn about the core parts of AngularJS. A series of examples will gradually showcase the main AngularJS features. After a high-level overview of the AngularJS architecture, a more complex example will be shown, allowing the reader to see how data binding works and how to respond to user events. The chapter will end with an overview of the JavaScript patterns that are essential for AngularJS applications, which will be followed by an overview of AngularJS building blocks.

*Chapter 2, Creating an AngularJS Client-side Application in Visual Studio*, teaches the reader how to use Visual Studio to build an AngularJS application. A walkthrough to set up the development environment using the AngularJS NuGet packages will be followed by a presentation of the workflow involved in building an AngularJS application and some of the best practices in organizing the project structure. The final topic will cover building a complex AngularJS application.

*Chapter 3, Creating .NET Web Services for AngularJS*, teaches the reader about RESTful web services, how to use a .NET web service framework that is a great fit for AngularJS, and how to create web service resources for AngularJS. A brief presentation of the REST principles will be followed by a discussion on why RESTful web services work very well with AngularJS. An overview of the .NET web services framework, ServiceStack, will evolve into a walkthrough to create the required web service resources that will be used in the AngularJS example from the previous chapter.

*Chapter 4, Creating an AngularJS, ASP.NET MVC, ServiceStack Application*, teaches the reader how to integrate an AngularJS application with ASP.NET MVC and ServiceStack and how to create a production-ready application. An overview of ASP.NET MVC will be followed by a discussion about when you need to combine ASP.NET MVC and AngularJS. A walkthrough of how to set up routing with ASP.NET MVC and how to secure AngularJS applications will be next and the chapter will conclude with presenting additional tasks needed for AngularJS and backend integration.

*Chapter 5, Testing and Debugging AngularJS Applications*, teaches the reader how to test and debug AngularJS components, test web services, and how to implement end-to-end testing. The next topics are a discussion about why it is important to test web service endpoints, how to test them, and what additional tasks are needed for IE 8 support.

*Chapter 6, Advanced AngularJS Topics*, teaches the reader about advanced topics such as internationalization, animations, JSONP and CORS considerations, and template caching.

# What you need for this book

The minimum software requirement is Visual Studio 2013 Express for Web and the recommended one is Visual Studio 2013 Professional. For testing and debugging AngularJS applications, you also need to install Node.js, Node.js Tools for Visual Studio, and Java SE Development Kit 7 (JDK 7).

# Who this book is for

The book is targeted at .NET developers who have already built web applications or web services and have a fundamental knowledge of HTML, JavaScript, and CSS.

# Conventions

In this book, you will find a number of styles of text that distinguish between different kinds of information. Here are some examples of these styles, and an explanation of their meaning.

Code words in text, database table names, folder names, filenames, file extensions, pathnames, dummy URLs, user input, and Twitter handles are shown as follows: "It will match some regular HTML tags such as `input` and `select` if they contain `ng-` prefixed attributes or CSS classes."

A block of code is set as follows:

```
var myAppModule = angular.module('myApp', []);
  myAppModule.controller('ExampleController', function ($scope) {
    $scope.name = "Alex Pop";
    $scope.previousName = "";
    $scope.onNameFocused = function() {
      $scope.previousName = $scope.name;
    };
  });
```

When we wish to draw your attention to a particular part of a code block, the relevant lines or items are set in bold:

```
var myAppModule = angular.module('myApp', []);
  myAppModule.controller('ExampleController', ['$scope', function
($scope) {
    $scope.name = "Alex Pop";
    $scope.previousName = "";
    $scope.onNameFocused = function() {
      $scope.previousName = $scope.name;
    };
```

Any command-line input or output is written as follows:

```
Install-Package AngularJS.Core -Version 1.2.15
```

**New terms** and **important words** are shown in bold. Words that you see on the screen, in menus or dialog boxes for example, appear in the text like this: "The main menu for our application will contain three links to the three main views: **Rentals**, **Customers**, and **Bicycles**."

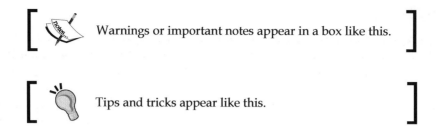

Warnings or important notes appear in a box like this.

Tips and tricks appear like this.

# Reader feedback

Feedback from our readers is always welcome. Let us know what you think about this book—what you liked or may have disliked. Reader feedback is important for us to develop titles that you really get the most out of.

To send us general feedback, simply send an e-mail to feedback@packtpub.com, and mention the book title via the subject of your message.

If there is a topic that you have expertise in and you are interested in either writing or contributing to a book, see our author guide on www.packtpub.com/authors.

# Customer support

Now that you are the proud owner of a Packt book, we have a number of things to help you to get the most from your purchase.

# Downloading the example code

You can download the example code files for all Packt books you have purchased from your account at http://www.packtpub.com. If you purchased this book elsewhere, you can visit http://www.packtpub.com/support and register to have the files e-mailed directly to you.

# Errata

Although we have taken every care to ensure the accuracy of our content, mistakes do happen. If you find a mistake in one of our books—maybe a mistake in the text or the code—we would be grateful if you would report this to us. By doing so, you can save other readers from frustration and help us improve subsequent versions of this book. If you find any errata, please report them by visiting http://www.packtpub.com/submit-errata, selecting your book, clicking on the **errata submission form** link, and entering the details of your errata. Once your errata are verified, your submission will be accepted and the errata will be uploaded on our website, or added to any list of existing errata, under the Errata section of that title. Any existing errata can be viewed by selecting your title from http://www.packtpub.com/support.

# Piracy

Piracy of copyright material on the Internet is an ongoing problem across all media. At Packt, we take the protection of our copyright and licenses very seriously. If you come across any illegal copies of our works, in any form, on the Internet, please provide us with the location address or website name immediately so that we can pursue a remedy.

Please contact us at copyright@packtpub.com with a link to the suspected pirated material.

We appreciate your help in protecting our authors, and our ability to bring you valuable content.

# Questions

You can contact us at questions@packtpub.com if you are having a problem with any aspect of the book, and we will do our best to address it.

# 1
# Introducing AngularJS

In this chapter, we will learn how to manipulate HTML using AngularJS and will also learn about the core parts of AngularJS. A series of examples will gradually showcase the main AngularJS features. After a high-level overview of the AngularJS architecture, more complex examples will be shown, allowing the reader to see how data binding works and how to respond to user events. The chapter will continue with an overview of the JavaScript patterns that are essential for AngularJS applications, followed by an overview of AngularJS building blocks. The list of topics explored in this chapter is as follows:

- Presenting AngularJS with examples
- Controllers
- An overview of the AngularJS architecture
- JavaScript patterns and practices for AngularJS
- Dependency injection
- Services
- Directives
- Filters

The version of AngularJS used in this book is 1.2 because it is the latest version that will support Internet Explorer 8. .NET developers often have to support corporate clients that use older Internet Explorer versions, and this needs to be taken into account when planning the AngularJS adoption. You will see references to AngularJS Version 1.2.15 throughout the book, but all of the code should be compatible with any newer 1.2.x version that is available when you are reading this material.

All of the code examples from this chapter are also hosted online with HTML, CSS, and JavaScript editors at `http://plnkr.co`. This editor is built with AngularJS and is a great tool to share examples and isolate frontend application parts when using collaboration sites such as `http://stackoverflow.com`. For convenience, the code from this book is also hosted on GitHub in two repositories: `http://github.com/popalexandruvasile/angularjs-dotnet-book` (for individual examples used to introduce specific concepts) and `http://github.com/popalexandruvasile/rentthatbike` (for the main application example that will be built incrementally throughout the book). The code for this chapter can also be found at `http://github.com/popalexandruvasile/angularjs-dotnet-book/tree/master/Chapter1`.

I recommend using the Google Chrome browser for the examples in this book. It has an extension called *AngularJS Batarang*, which will reveal additional information about the AngularJS objects loaded in the current browser session. When using this extension on `http://plnkr.co`, you need to open the example in a separate browser window for best results. This extension will be explored in *Chapter 5, Testing and Debugging AngularJS Applications*, so that you can use the details mentioned there to set it up.

Before discussing AngularJS, it is worth mentioning that this framework comes with online documentation in the form of a developer guide at `http://code.angularjs.org/1.2.15/docs/guide`, and its API is documented at `http://code.angularjs.org/1.2.15/docs/api`. As this book is not an in-depth guide to AngularJS, you might find these links useful to gain more insight into the concepts and API explored here.

# Presenting AngularJS with examples

The best way to present AngularJS is to explore a couple of examples first. I will then introduce the key AngularJS concepts showcased in these examples.

## A jQuery example

Let's compare and contrast an example of a web page built with jQuery against an example of the same page built with AngularJS. The web page allows the user to enter a name and select a favorite color, and it will display formatted markup that reflects the entered values. The end result is shown in the next screenshot:

The following first code example is jQuery-based, with initial HTML content and additional behavior injected into the $(document).ready() event:

```
<!DOCTYPE html>
<html>
<head>
  <meta charset="utf-8" />
  <title>Chapter1 Example1</title>
  <script src="http://code.jquery.com/jquery-
1.11.0.min.js"></script>
</head>
<body>
  <h1>Introduction</h1>
  <label>My name:</label>
  <input id="input-name" type="text" placeholder="Please enter
name" />
  <br />
  <label>My favorite color:</label>
  <select id="select-color">
    <option>Please select</option>
    <option>red</option>
    <option>yellow</option>
    <option>magenta</option>
  </select>
```

```
    <h3 id="heading-name" style="display:none">Hello! My name is
<span id="span-name"></span>.</h3>
    <h3 id="heading-color" style="display:none">
    My favorite color is <span id="span-
color">  </span>.</h3>
<script>
    $(document).ready(function() {
      $("#input-name").keyup(function() {
        var name = $("#input-name").val();
        if (name) {
          $("#span-name").text(name);
          $("#heading-name").show();
        } else {
          $("#heading-name").hide();
        }
      });
      $("#select-color").change(function() {
        var color = $("#select-color").val();
        if (color != "Please select") {
          $("#span-color").css('background-color', color);
          $("#span-color").attr('title', color);
          $("#heading-color").show();
        } else {
          $("#heading-color").hide();
        }
      });
    });
</script>
</body>
</html>
```

You can view the preceding example either online at `http://plnkr.co/edit/6wJ10DpmGhLIyWMxI3eP` or in the `Example1` folder from the source code for this chapter.

You will notice in the preceding example that we had to prepare the HTML markup for jQuery integration by having the `id` attributes set for specific elements. The JavaScript code binds to element events and will react to changes in user input, displaying the formatted content for valid entries and hiding it for invalid ones. JavaScript code is separated from HTML content, and the number of lines for each section is comparable.

# An AngularJS example

The second example shown in the following code is based on AngularJS, and the functionality is identical to the previous example (try to ignore the highlighted element attributes for the moment, and the variables surrounded by curly brackets will be discussed later in this book):

```
<!DOCTYPE html>
<html ng-app>
<head>
  <meta charset="utf-8" />
  <title>Chapter1 Example2</title>
  <script
src="http://code.angularjs.org/1.2.14/angular.js"></script>
</head>
<body>
  <h1>Introduction</h1>
  <label>My name:</label>
  <input type="text" placeholder="Please enter name" ng-
model="name">
  <br/>
  <label>My favorite color:</label>
  <select ng-model="color">
    <option value="">Please select</option>
    <option>red</option>
    <option>yellow</option>
    <option>magenta</option>
  </select>
  <h3 ng-show="name">Hello! My name is {{name}}.</h3>
  <h3 ng-show="color">My favourite color is
  <span title="{{color}}" style="background-
color:{{color}};">  </span>.</h3>
</body>
</html>
```

You can view the preceding example either online at http://plnkr.co/edit/yQ3WAJ8XKwtaFDnKWiCU or in the Example2 folder from the source code for this chapter. If you executed the previous example, you might have noticed a slight delay between when the name was entered and when it was displayed further down the page. This delay disappears in the AngularJS example due to its faster DOM manipulation.

You will notice that the HTML section does not have any id element attribute set, and there is no JavaScript code section. The only JavaScript reference is to the AngularJS core file that links to the current stable version of the framework. There are new element attributes, all prefixed with ng-. This prefix marks the built-in AngularJS extensions to the HTML vocabulary, also known as directives, and this prefix will appear often in the HTML code snippets throughout this book. This approach to extend the HTML markup by defining new element attributes, or even new elements, transforms it into meaningful and expressive markup, which is one of the major differentiating factors from a jQuery-based approach or from other JavaScript frameworks. By removing the boilerplate code from the jQuery example, AngularJS allows the developer to be more productive and use markup instead of code as much as possible. It also enables the sharing of HTML markup with a designer in a collaborative workflow, where HTML markup and JavaScript code are loosely coupled and not linked as tightly together as in the jQuery example through special element identifiers and CSS classes.

The first AngularJS-specific, most distinctive HTML attribute is ng-app. It sets the boundaries of the AngularJS application and can be applied on any HTML element, with the only constraint being that it can appear only once. The HTML element with the ng-app attribute is the AngularJS application root element. AngularJS will parse the markup delimited by the application root element and look for any ng- prefixed elements, attributes, or CSS classes. It will match some regular HTML tags such as input and select if they contain ng- prefixed attributes or CSS classes. These entities will then be mapped to instances of special AngularJS components called directives.

The directives are used to add dynamic behavior to HTML content and introduce a powerful, versatile, and declarative user interface definition language. Even the initial ng-app attribute maps to a directive used to bootstrap the AngularJS application. The next highlighted attribute in the example is ng-model. This attribute introduces the concept of **scope**, the fundamental data model in AngularJS.

All HTML elements in an AngularJS application will be associated with at least one instance of an object called scope. Scope is the special ingredient that links the view, as represented by HTML elements, to the code behind the view, represented in this example by directives. The scope object is initialized and owned by AngularJS components, and the view can only reference properties and functions of the scope object.

The application root element will be associated with the initial scope of the application. This initial scope is called the root scope, and any AngularJS application will have at least one scope: the instance of the root scope. Since some directives have their own scope instance created for them implicitly, a typical AngularJS application will have a hierarchy of scopes, with the root scope at the top.

Going back to the AngularJS example, the first `ng-model` attribute maps the value of the current `input` element to a property on the current scope instance. In our case, this specific property is the `name` property of the root scope. The `name` property is not defined anywhere prior to the `ng-model` attribute, and it will be created implicitly for the underlying scope instance by AngularJS. The mechanism where the value of a scope property and the value of an HTML element can update each other is called two-way data binding, and its signature in AngularJS is the `ng-model` attribute.

The next highlighted `ng-model` attribute maps the value of the `select` element to a new property of the current scope called `color`. The attribute is used in two different HTML elements, and its effect is similar—as soon as the user enters their name or selects a color, the changed values get stored as distinct properties on the current scope instance.

This concludes the data entry part of the example. The next part is about data display, and we start with the highlighted `ng-show` attribute. To understand the functionality introduced here, we have to discuss AngularJS expressions first.

An AngularJS expression is similar to a JavaScript expression used in the `eval()` function call. It is always evaluated against the current scope, and it can reference a scope property or more scope properties linked by logical operators. An AngularJS expression will ignore null or undefined scope properties, and this is another important difference from an equivalent JavaScript expression. In our example, the `ng-show` expression would not have generated an exception if the `name` scope property had not been defined previously.

The directive introduced by the `ng-show` attribute will show or hide its HTML element depending on the true or false evaluation of the expression from the attribute value. When the `name` property gets a nonempty value following user text input, then the first `h3` element is displayed.

The next highlighted HTML snippet is `{{name}}`. This represents an interpolation that is based on an AngularJS expression that will be evaluated against the scope object and displayed as text inside the `h3` tag. Interpolation is similar to one-way data binding from other templating systems, and it has the same outcome of a code expression being transformed into a string. The difference is that interpolation can use any valid AngularJS expression, and it accepts a value like `{{name + ' and I am explaining Example2'}}`.

The interpolation expression will reflect a change in the `name` scope property following user text input. We can start to visualize the flow of data from the `input` element through AngularJS and back to the `h3` element.

The second h3 element is similar to the first one and bound to the color scope property instead. The first binding expression is an attribute value, and the second one is part of an attribute value. The fact that we can have a binding on HTML content—text, attribute, and even element tag—shows the power and versatility of AngularJS.

The following diagram shows the data flow from Example2:

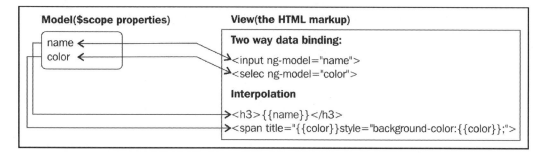

The preceding diagram mentions the model and view as the two distinct concepts associated with the data binding and interpolation mechanism, and they will be explored in detail after we discuss the next AngularJS component.

# Introducing the AngularJS controller

We will expand the previous example to include additional logic. The example will count how many times the color was changed, and it will display the count when it is greater than one, as shown in the following screenshot:

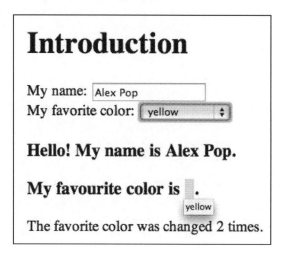

The following example contains new AngularJS directives and components that support the additional logic, as highlighted:

```html
<!DOCTYPE html>
<html ng-app>
<head>
  <meta charset="utf-8" />
  <title>Chapter1 Example3</title>
  <script
src="http://code.angularjs.org/1.2.14/angular.js"></script>
</head>
<body ng-controller="ExampleController">
  <h1>Introduction</h1>
  <label>My name:</label>
  <input type="text" placeholder="Please enter name" ng-
model="name">
  <br/>
  <label>My favorite color:</label>
  <select ng-model="color" ng-change="onColorChanged()">
    <option value="">Please select</option>
    <option>red</option>
    <option>yellow</option>
    <option>magenta</option>
  </select>
  <h3 ng-show="name">Hello! My name is {{name}}.</h3>
  <h3 ng-show="color">My favourite color is
  <span title="{{color}}" style="background-
color:{{color}};">  </span>.</h3>
  <div ng-show="colorChangeCount > 0">The favorite color was
changed {{colorChangeCount}} times.</div>
<script>
  function ExampleController($scope) {
    $scope.colorChangeCount = 0;
    $scope.onColorChanged = function() {
      $scope.colorChangeCount++;
    };
  }
</script>
</body>
</html>
```

You can view the preceding example either online at `http://plnkr.co/` `edit/5xW4MplFbcnTzMeOljov` or in the `Example3` folder from the source code for this chapter.

The first highlighted attribute, `ng-controller`, introduces a directive that maps an AngularJS object called controller to the HTML section delimited by the current element. The controller is defined in the highlighted `script` tag as a globally accessible function. We call this function the controller constructor function. Note the `$scope` parameter that represents the current scope instance. This parameter gets initialized automatically by AngularJS, so when the controller constructor function is executed, the scope is available and ready to use. Declaring a parameter in a component definition and expecting AngularJS to automatically provide it is the signature of the dependency injection mechanism, which will be explored in detail in this chapter.

The scope passed to the controller is also attached to the view represented by the HTML element with the `ng-controller` attribute. The controller and view share data through the model represented by the scope instance. Any property defined on the controller scope will also be visible to the HTML view.

The first scope property is `colorChangeCount`. The second property is the `onColorChanged` function, which increments `colorChangeCount` when called. The two properties are a typical example of the custom logic found in an AngularJS controller.

Going back to the HTML from the previous example, the next highlighted snippet is the attribute, `ng-change`. This maps to a directive that will evaluate the expression value of the attribute every time the selection changes. This directive can also be used with `input` elements and requires the existence of the `ng-model` attribute. In our example, the `ng-change` attribute value is the `onColorChanged()` expression. AngularJS expressions might contain function calls, which are convenient when the expression being evaluated is too long or complex to be used as an attribute value.

This wraps up the data entry section of the controller logic. Next, we move on to the data visualization part, and you will notice that the first scope property is referenced by the HTML view in an `ng-show` attribute and in the `{{colorChangeCount}}` binding. The directive mapped to `ng-show` evaluates the property when changed, and a subsequent message is displayed if the property value is greater than zero or otherwise hidden.

I have updated the previous diagram for `Example2` to reflect only what has been changed in `Example3`, as follows:

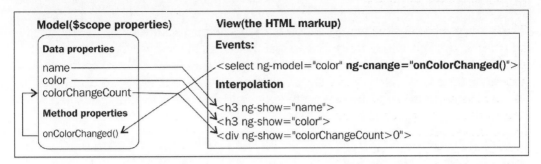

The darker arrows show the flow of data from the view to the model via the `onColorChanged()` method triggered by the `select` element change event. The model is updated in this method, and the change flows back to the view again through the `colorChangeCount` property. Note how the controller is not explicitly mentioned here as it does not have an active role in the data binding mechanism in AngularJS other than initializing the model represented by scope data properties and methods.

Another mechanism worth mentioning is the **dirty checking** process where AngularJS detects changes triggered by user interaction and propagates them as part of the scope life cycle by calling the `scope.$apply` method. Changes that occurred in scope properties or that have an effect on any expression are propagated within the `scope.$digest` method, which is called at the end of the `$apply` method. Any controller or directive can observe the changes in scope properties using the `scope.$watch` method, and these changes are propagated when the `scope.$digest` method is called as part of the scope life cycle.

 You can find more information on the scope life cycle and how changes are detected and propagated by AngularJS at `http://code.angularjs.org/1.2.15/docs/guide/scope`.

We now have a full working example that showcases the key concepts from AngularJS with the controller as the main vehicle to implement business logic and react to user input through the scope methods. It is now time to reveal the concepts underlying the first AngularJS examples in the next section.

# An overview of the AngularJS architecture

The code for `Example1` from the previous section was focused on jQuery and is representative of the JavaScript code that was at large when AngularJS was created. The example code has the manipulation of HTML elements intertwined with business logic. This makes it difficult to test the business logic in isolation from the presentation logic. Any change in application data or user input has to be manually propagated back and forth to the view represented by HTML elements. Compared to the AngularJS example, there is a lot more code that needs to be written, and this code might be difficult to scale and reuse.

JavaScript frameworks such as Backbone.js, knockout.js, AngularJS, and others addressed the problems of scalability, reusability, and testability by embracing a design pattern traditionally used by server-side frameworks. This pattern is called **Model-View-Controller (MVC)**, and it is an established pattern that was originally introduced in the 1970s. You should already be familiar with it from the ASP.NET MVC fundamentals, but I will revisit it here for reference.

 Technically, AngularJS uses a variant of the MVC, which is closer to the **Model-View-ViewModel (MVVM)** pattern, but the definition of MVC from the next section still applies to it. One of the core members of the AngularJS team declared the main design pattern behind AngularJS as being "Model-View-Whatever works for you" (MVW or MV*) in this post at `http://plus.google.com/+AngularJS/posts/aZNVhj355G2`.

# The Model-View-Controller pattern

The design pattern is specific for applications with user interfaces and introduces a separation between the following aspects:

- **Model**: This is the application data and the business logic associated with it
- **View**: This is the output of the application data in any form that can be consumed or manipulated by a user
- **Controller**: This is the logic to get data from the View to the Model and back, and to manage any interaction with the View or the Model

The Model does not have direct access to the View or Controller. Any change in the Model gets propagated to the View through notifications or polling by the Controller. This allows the Model to be tested in isolation from the View and Controller. It supports the separation of concerns between application layers, which is essential to support code reusability and scalability. You can reuse the same model to power different views or cache model instances between application data requests.

The Controller can be instantiated without requiring the underlying View infrastructure to be active. This ensures Controller testability, and it hides the specifics of the View infrastructure implementation from the Controller. You can reuse the same Controller to power different Views with a similar structure and functionality or to power Views that differ only through the infrastructure implementation.

I mentioned the Model, View, and Controller concepts in the previous section, and I identified them as follows:

- **Model**: This contains the scope properties. Any directive or controller has access to a scope instance.
- **View**: This contains the rendered HTML elements that are enhanced or extended by directives.
- **Controller**: This is a constructor function that has access to a scope instance and uses it to provide data and functions to the View.

The MVC pattern, as used in AngularJS, allows a great degree of flexibility for the application code. It introduces the reusability of Controllers, Models and, Views; you can have the same Controller reused for multiple Views, the same Model reused in multiple Controllers, and the same View reused for multiple Controllers. It also adds testability for Models, Controllers, and even directives. Understanding how the pattern needs to be used in AngularJS is key to organizing your application code.

If we go back to Example3, we will be able to identify the $scope parameter of the ExampleController function with the Model, the markup delimited by the body element and the ng-controller attribute with the View, and the ExampleController function with the Controller.

# The structure of an AngularJS application

The examples from the previous section use an implicit application configuration. There are examples when you need to run some configuration before the application starts, or you need to run multiple AngularJS applications from a single JavaScript code base.

## Bootstrapping an AngularJS application

The framework allows for an explicit application initialization, as showcased in the next example. I reduced the first AngularJS example, and it now allows only username editing. I added a new attribute, ng-focus, which is a directive that will evaluate an expression when the input element is focused.

The code executed in the following event will show the previously entered username while the new username is being changed:

```html
<!DOCTYPE html>
<html ng-app="myApp">
<head>
  <meta charset="utf-8" />
  <title>Chapter1 Example4</title>
  <script
src="http://code.angularjs.org/1.2.14/angular.js"></script>
</head>
<body ng-controller="ExampleController">
  <h1>Introduction</h1>
  <label>My name:</label>
  <input type="text" placeholder="Please enter name" ng-
model="name" ng-focus="onNameFocused()">
  <h3 ng-show="name">Hello! My name is {{name}}.</h3>
  <div ng-show="previousName">Previous name was
{{previousName}}.</div>
<script>
  var myAppModule = angular.module('myApp', []);
  myAppModule.controller('ExampleController', function ($scope) {
    $scope.name = "Alex Pop";
    $scope.previousName = "";
    $scope.onNameFocused = function() {
      $scope.previousName = $scope.name;
    };
  });
</script>
</body>
</html>
```

You can view the example either online at http://plnkr.co/edit/ dfJKeNwuRMweGveBhErE or in the Example4 folder from the source code for this chapter.

The first highlighted attribute is ng-app, which has a value this time around. The myApp value represents the unique identifier of the current AngularJS application. The next highlighted code initializes a new AngularJS component called module, which will be used via the myApp identifier to bootstrap the AngularJS application.

A module is a container-like object with a unique identifier that groups together the AngularJS components used to build an application: controllers, directives, and others, such as providers, factories, services, values, constants, animations, and filters. The module has methods that are specific to the AngularJS application components I mentioned. You can see one of these methods in the last highlighted code section in the previous example.

The module `controller` function takes the controller name and controller constructor function as arguments. The constructor function is similar to the one from `Example3`, and this time around, it is associated with a specific module rather than being standalone. Throughout this chapter, we will explore other module methods when we introduce AngularJS components.

# Defining module dependencies

Modules can be used to share AngularJS components between different applications. A module can reference other modules, as in the following example, showing a different module definition:

```
var myApp1Module = angular.module('myApp1', ['myApp2', 'myApp3']);
```

The second parameter of the module definition is the array of module names that the application depends on. The AngularJS framework itself is organized into different modules. The principal AngularJS module is called `ng`, and it is loaded into every AngularJS application by default. Other AngularJS modules, such as `ngResource`, that provide functionality for web services have to be explicitly referenced and declared as a dependency of the application. First, you need to reference the JavaScript file that contains the `ngResource` module as shown in the following code:

```
<script src="http://code.angularjs.org/1.2.14/angular-
resource.js"></script>
```

Then, you need to declare a dependency on the module for the AngularJS application using the following code:

```
var myAppModule = angular.module('myApp', ['ngResource']);
```

A similar procedure has to be implemented if you want to perform the following tasks:

- Split your application into different modules. By doing so, you can reuse the modules between different AngularJS applications.

- Reference other AngularJS framework modules such as `ngRoute` or third-party AngularJS modules such as AngularUI Bootstrap `ui.bootstrap`.

The module dependency array is another signature of the dependency injection mechanism, explored later in this chapter, where the dependency names are declared, and AngularJS ensures that they are located, initialized, and provided to the application module.

A module has two methods that can be used to perform further configuration and initialization outside of individual AngularJS components. The first method is config, which allows you to perform any additional configuration when the module is loading. The second method is run, which allows you to run custom code after all of the module components are loaded.

# The JavaScript patterns and practices used in AngularJS applications

At this point, we are almost ready to discuss AngularJS in more detail. However, before doing that, we need to introduce some JavaScript patterns and practices that will be useful in understanding the rest of the content in this chapter.

One of the difficult problems to solve when writing JavaScript code is to avoid the pollution of the global scope. Any variable declared outside of a function body will automatically be visible to the global scope. You can easily imagine a scenario where your variable names clash with the variables defined in other JavaScript files or libraries. Also, JavaScript automatically moves all variable declarations to the top of the current scope. This behavior is called "hoisting" and can lead to scenarios where you use a variable before it is declared, which is confusing and can cause unintended errors.

To avoid these problems, a typical workaround is to use a function body to declare your variables. Variables declared in this way belong to the local scope of the current function, and they are invisible to the global scope. This workaround is based on two patterns used frequently in AngularJS code bases: the **Immediately-invoked Function Expression (IIFE)**—pronounced "iffy"—and the revealing module pattern.

## Immediately-invoked Function Expression

If we append the line, console.log(myAppModule.name); at the end of the script section from the full example of the previous AngularJS application, we will see the name of the module written in the console as **myApp**. If we convert the example to use an Immediately-invoked Function Expression, the script section will look like the following code:

```
;(function(){
  var myAppModule = angular.module('myApp', []);
  myAppModule.controller('ExampleController', function ($scope) {
    $scope.name = "Alex Pop";
```

```
      $scope.previousName = "";
      $scope.onNameFocused = function() {
        $scope.previousName = $scope.name;
      };
    });
  }());
  console.log(myAppModule.name);
```

You can view the preceding example either online at `http://plnkr.co/edit/`
`A6XZfvgJITpctLEwmXC7` or in the `Example5` folder from the source code
for this chapter.

I have highlighted the changes required to convert the code to use the
Immediately-invoked Function Expression. The leading semicolon prevents
issues caused by the automatic semicolon insertions in JavaScript when your
scripts get concatenated with other scripts. The enclosing parentheses after the
leading semicolon and before the last semicolon are a convention for these types
of expressions.

The example will still work as before, but the console output will have this message:
**Uncaught ReferenceError: myAppModule is not defined**. Using this pattern, we
made the application module invisible to the global scope, while leaving it accessible
to the AngularJS infrastructure.

# The revealing module pattern

The revealing module pattern solves the problem of implementation details being
hidden for JavaScript objects that need to provide publicly accessible properties.
The following example is a plain JavaScript one—no external library references
are required:

```
<!DOCTYPE html>
<html>
<head>
  <meta charset="utf-8" />
  <title>Chapter1 Example6</title>
</head>
<body>
  <h1>Revealing module pattern</h1>
  <script>
    var revealingModule = (function() {
      var innerObject = 5;
      var innerFunction = function(value) {
```

```
        return innerObject + value;
      };
      return {
        outerObject1: innerFunction(1),
        outerObject2: innerFunction(2),
        outerFunction: innerFunction
      };
    }());
    console.log("outerObject1:" + revealingModule.outerObject1);
    console.log("outerObject2:" + revealingModule.outerObject2);
    console.log("innerObject:" + revealingModule.innerObject);
    console.log("outerFunction(3):" +
revealingModule.outerFunction(3));
    console.log("innerFunction(3):" +
revealingModule.innerFunction(3));
  </script>
</body>
</html>
```

You can view the example either online at `http://plnkr.co/edit/ AFbIj5YQO64N9sKYF19u` or in the `Example6` folder from the source code for this chapter.

I have highlighted the revealing module pattern, and you will notice that it relies on an IIFE to define itself. Using this pattern, all of the variables declared inside of the IIFE are inaccessible to the outside scope, and the only visible properties are the ones returned in the last statement. The console output for this example is the following:

```
outerObject1:6
outerObject2:7
innerObject:undefined
outerFunction(3):8
Uncaught TypeError: Object #<Object> has no method 'innerFunction'
```

Any reference to the variables defined within the IIFE will be unsuccessful, even if the property exposed is a direct reference to an inner variable like the `outerFunction` property. You will see this pattern in action throughout the rest of the examples of this book.

You can find more information about the revealing module pattern and other JavaScript design patterns in the online resource *Learning JavaScript Design Patterns, Addy Osmani, O'Reilly Media,* available at `http://addyosmani.com/ resources/essentialjsdesignpatterns/book`.

# The strict mode of JavaScript

The JavaScript standard ECMAScript 5 has introduced a new way to use a stricter variant of JavaScript. This variant changes the behavior of the JavaScript runtime, and the following are some changes that occur in strict mode:

- Some silent errors are thrown instead of being ignored, such as assignment to a nonwritable property.

- All global variables need to be explicitly declared. When you mistype a global variable name, an exception is thrown.

- All of the property names of an object need to be unique, and all of the parameter names for a function also need to be unique.

By including the line `"use strict";` in your scripts, you can adhere to the ECMAScript 5 strict mode when using a modern browser. If the script is loaded in an older browser, the statement is ignored and the JavaScript is parsed in non-strict mode. Strict mode can only be safely declared at the top of a function body. If it is declared in the global scope, it can cause issues when a strict mode script is concatenated with other non-strict scripts.

Using strict mode leads to safer, cleaner code with fewer errors. It is now common practice that any AngularJS script will be enclosed by an IIFE with strict mode enabled.

All AngularJS examples throughout the rest of the book will use the patterns discussed in this section.

# Dependency injection

When I introduced the controller, I mentioned the fact that the AngularJS infrastructure initializes and loads the `$scope` object. The controller constructor function that uses the application module is shown in the following code:

```
var myAppModule = angular.module('myApp', []);
  myAppModule.controller('ExampleController', function ($scope) {
    $scope.name = "Alex Pop";
    $scope.previousName = "";
    $scope.onNameFocused = function() {
      $scope.previousName = $scope.name;
    };
  });
```

I highlighted the controller constructor function. It has the $scope parameter specified, but it has not been initialized anywhere. You will see this type of function signature a lot for AngularJS controllers and other object definitions. A controller declares its dependencies (such as the $scope parameter) in its constructor function signature, and AngularJS uses a technique called **dependency injection** to manage and load these dependencies.

Dependency injection is a software design pattern that facilitates the management of code dependencies by delegating them to a dedicated software component known as the **injector**. Each AngularJS module has an injector instance that deals with resolving controllers and other object dependencies by loading all object definitions before the application starts and injecting them as parameters to constructor functions during application runtime.

In the previous example, the controller definition uses **implicit dependency injection**. The AngularJS injector looks at the parameter name and infers the required dependency that needs to be resolved, which is the current available $scope instance. However, if your JavaScript code gets minified as part of the build process, the parameter name will be changed and the injector will not be able to infer the correct name. For this scenario, you need to use **explicit dependency injection** as highlighted in the next example:

```
var myAppModule = angular.module('myApp', []);
  myAppModule.controller('ExampleController', ['$scope', function
($scope) {
    $scope.name = "Alex Pop";
    $scope.previousName = "";
    $scope.onNameFocused = function() {
      $scope.previousName = $scope.name;
    };
```

You can view the example either online at `http://plnkr.co/edit/rbd1GjPEK1OGrnPGFsjg` or in the `Example7` folder from the source code for this chapter.

The constructor function was replaced with an array that contains the dependency names with the constructor function as the last element. It is good practice to use explicit dependency injection, and we will use it throughout the rest of the AngularJS examples in this book.

# Introducing AngularJS services

Until this point, we have discussed some of the core concepts of the AngularJS architecture. The content we covered so far should be a good starter for very small applications or other scenarios where we just need to use out of the box AngularJS directives and other built-in components.

For other types of applications or more advanced usage scenarios, we will sometimes need to reuse code or share data between two or more controllers. Let's take the previous AngularJS example and change it from a user introduction screen to a game setup screen. The screen will now allow the editing of two player names while keeping track of the previous names. To provide this functionality, I have created two separate controllers, each one with access to its own scope instance. The following code is the content of the body element:

```
<h1>Game setup</h1>
<div ng-controller="ExampleController1">
  <h2>Player 1</h2>
  <label>Name:</label>
  <input type="text" placeholder="Please enter player 1 name"
ng-model="name" ng-focus="onNameFocused()">
  <h3 ng-show="name">Player 1 name is {{name}}.</h3>
  <h3 ng-show="previousName">Previous Player 1 name was
{{previousName}}.</h3>
</div>
<div ng-controller="ExampleController2">
  <h2>Player 2</h2>
  <label>Name:</label>
  <input type="text" placeholder="Please enter player 2 name"
ng-model="name" ng-focus="onNameFocused()">
  <h3 ng-show="name">Player 2 name is {{name}}.</h3>
  <h3 ng-show="previousName">Previous Player 2 name was
{{previousName}}.</h3>
</div>
<script>
 (function(){
  "use strict";
  var myAppModule = angular.module('myApp', []);
  myAppModule.controller('ExampleController1', ['$scope', function
($scope) {
```

```
      $scope.name = "Player1";
      $scope.previousName = "";
      $scope.onNameFocused = function() {
        $scope.previousName = $scope.name;
      };
    }]);
    myAppModule.controller('ExampleController2', ['$scope', function
  ($scope) {
      $scope.name = "Player2";
      $scope.previousName = "";
      $scope.onNameFocused = function() {
        $scope.previousName = $scope.name;
      };
    }]);
  }());
</script>
```

You can view the example either online at `http://plnkr.co/edit/` `e8oWZu68tMwsGAbHDUEN` or in the `Example8` folder from the source code for this chapter.

I have highlighted the directives that associate the two controllers with HTML elements. The code of the two controllers is almost identical, with the exception of the initial player name value. It looks like unnecessary code duplication, but fortunately, AngularJS has a built-in component that allows us to refactor and reuse this code. This built-in component is called a **service**, and it is defined using a syntax similar to a controller definition.

Usually, we register a service with an AngularJS application module that uses a service factory function. This function will be called by AngularJS to create the service instance that will be used throughout the AngularJS application. This service instance will be injected in all AngularJS components that declare a dependency on the particular service. The following example uses a service factory function to define a service that encapsulates the code shared between the controllers from the previous example. The following code is the content of the body element with the HTML markup placed first:

```
    <h1>Game setup</h1>
    <div ng-controller="ExampleController1">
      <h2>Player 1</h2>
      <label>Name:</label>
      <input type="text" placeholder="Please enter player 1 name"
  ng-model="player.name" ng-focus="player.onNameFocused()">
      <h3 ng-show="player.name">Player 1 name is
  {{player.name}}.</h3>
```

```
    <h3 ng-show="player.previousName">Previous Player 1 name was
{{player.previousName}}.</h3>
  </div>
  <div ng-controller="ExampleController2">
    <h2>Player 2</h2>
    <label>Name:</label>
    <input type="text" placeholder="Please enter player 2 name"
ng-model="player.name" ng-focus="player.onNameFocused()">
    <h3 ng-show="player.name">Player 2 name is
{{player.name}}.</h3>
    <h3 ng-show="player.previousName">Previous Player 2 name was
{{player.previousName}}.</h3>
    <h3>Player count across all service instances is
{{playerCount}}.</h3>
  </div>
```

The markup now references the $scope data model through a new player object as highlighted in the HTML for Player 1. Let's take a look at the script section, where I have highlighted the new service definition in the following code:

```
<script>
  (function() {
    "use strict";
    var myAppModule = angular.module('myApp', []);
    myAppModule.factory('playerService', function() {
      var playerCount = 0;
      var createDefaultPlayer = function() {
        playerCount += 1;
        var player = {
          name: "",
          previousName: ""
        };
        player.onNameFocused = function() {
          player.previousName = player.name;
        };
        return player;
      };
      return {
        createPlayer: function(name) {
          var player = createDefaultPlayer();
          player.name = name;
          return player;
        },
```

```
        getPlayerCount: function() {
          return playerCount;
        }
      };
    });
    myAppModule.controller('ExampleController1', ['$scope',
'playerService',
      function($scope, playerService) {
        $scope.player = playerService.createPlayer('Player1');
      }
    ]);
    myAppModule.controller('ExampleController2', ['$scope',
'playerService',
      function($scope, playerService) {
        $scope.player = playerService.createPlayer('Player2');
        $scope.playerCount = playerService.getPlayerCount();
      }
    ]);
  }());
</script>
```

You can view the example either online at `http://plnkr.co/edit/OOocE8UUg1NWZLHidjmt` or in the `Example9` folder from the source code for this chapter.

The first highlighted snippet is the service definition that looks similar to a controller definition, with the exception that it returns an object that represents the service factory. This object is used to create the service instance that will be injected in all of the AngularJS components that have this service declared as a dependency.

In the new service, we transformed the previous controller code into a function called `createDefaultPlayer()`, which will create a new object that represents a player. The service instance has a method to create a new player with a predefined name called `createPlayer(name)`. The service factory function will keep track of how many player objects were created using the `playerCount` variable. The variable will be returned by the service instance function, `getPlayerCount()`. On a side note, you can see the revealing module pattern in action here. Although the script section is now bigger, we obtained new features such as code reusability and flexibility to provide more complex functionality than before.

There are other methods available on the module interface to declare an AngularJS service, such as `service`, `value`, and `constant`. The `service` method will use a constructor function to create the service instance, while the `value` method will use an already created service instance that will be passed unchanged to the AngularJS injector. The `constant` method is similar with the `value` method, with the difference that it will be available during the configuration phase of the application module. The `factory` method is one of the most flexible methods, and it will be the most frequently used method in the rest of the examples from this book. It allows additional configuration to the returned service instance, and you can even keep track of data outside of the service instance, such as with the `playerCount` variable from the previous example.

All service definition methods are, in fact, helpers of a more generic module method called `provider`. The method is a constructor function that creates an object that has to implement a `$get` method. The `$get` method returns a service factory function that will be used to create service instances by the injector. Usually, you need to use the `provider` method only when you need different configuration options for services reused across more than one application module. All service definition methods are ultimately resolved as `provider` methods by AngularJS. There is a `$provide` service that manages all objects created by this method, and these objects are called service providers. The `$injector` service uses the service providers to get the service instances that it needs to inject throughout an application module. You can get more information on service providers at `http://code.angularjs.org/1.2.15/docs/guide/providers`.

At this point, you will notice a naming convention among the service names prefixed with the $ symbol. This is an AngularJS-specific convention, where all of the services and special objects that belong to its infrastructure will be prefixed with the $ symbol. This helps developers identify their own services and components from AngularJS ones. It is worth mentioning that services can have dependencies on other services that are either built-in or custom, such as the one in the previous example.

The second highlighted code section is the new constructor function signature for the first controller. You will notice that we can now reference the new service alongside the `$scope` parameter using the explicit dependency injection notation. Both controllers are now using the same service instance. The last controller even displays the count of the player instances created by the service.

# Directives

One of the most important features of AngularJS is that it has majorly improved the HTML authoring story. It has extended the HTML vocabulary through directives, enabling a declarative style of defining the user interface. You can use its powerful, built-in directives and easily define new ones.

We have used a lot of directives in the examples presented so far, and most of them used the ng- prefix. When you take a look at the directives' documentation pages at http://code.angularjs.org/1.2.15/docs/api, you will notice that the directive names appear slightly different—ng-app is ngApp and ng-controller is ngController. AngularJS removes any data- or x- prefixes from the HTML markup and converts the -, _, and : characters to a camel case directive name. From now on, we will refer to different directives using the names from the AngularJS documentation.

# The ngRepeat directive

Next, we will explore some important built-in directives and see how to build custom directives. Looking back at the previous example, the HTML markup seems to have been duplicated for the two players. There is a built-in directive called ngRepeat that allows us to remove the duplicated markup as highlighted in the next example. The following code is the inclusive content of the body element without the script element:

```
<body ng-controller="ExampleController">
  <h1>Game setup</h1>
  <div ng-repeat="player in players">
    <h2>Player {{$index + 1}}</h2>
    <label>Name:</label>
    <input type="text" placeholder="Please enter player {{$index +
1}} name" ng-model="player.name" ng-
focus="player.onNameFocused()">
    <h3 ng-show="player.name">Player {{$index + 1}} name is
{{player.name}}.</h3>
    <h3 ng-show="player.previousName">Previous Player {{$index +
1}} name was {{player.previousName}}.</h3>
  </div>
</body>
```

You can view the example either online at http://plnkr.co/ edit/4tVY2Li9DjIg8LBqL3nK or in the Example10 folder from the source code for this chapter.

The ngRepeat directive works with a collection of objects and repeats an HTML markup section for each item in the collection. We created an array of player items in the controller that is used in the ngRepeat directive. The first highlighted code section shows the expression used to iterate through the collection, and the div element that has the directive is repeated for each item in the collection. The player variable defined in the ngRepeat expression is only available inside of the directive. The ngRepeat directive has its own scope that contains other directive-specific variables such as $index, which has been used in the next highlighted code snippet. This variable of the type number keeps track of the current collection item index, and there are other directive-specific Boolean variables available: $first, $middle, $last, $odd, and $even.

The example works for HTML markup that repeats a single element. When the HTML markup that needs repeated elements has separate start and end elements, you need to use two different directive attributes. The first is ng-repeat-start, which is a renamed ng-repeat directive that needs to be used on the start HTML element. The second is ng-repeat-end, which does not have an expression value and is used on the HTML element that ends the markup that needs repeated elements. The previous example of the body element content can now be written using the h2 element as the start of the repeated markup and the h3 element as the end, as shown in the following code:

```
<h1>Game setup</h1>
  <div>
    <h2 ng-repeat-start="player in players">Player {{$index +
1}}</h2>
    <label>Name:</label>
    <input type="text" placeholder="Please enter player {{$index +
1}} name" ng-model="player.name" ng-
focus="player.onNameFocused()">
    <h3 ng-show="player.name">Player {{$index + 1}} name is
{{player.name}}.</h3>
    <h3 ng-repeat-end ng-show="player.previousName">Previous
Player {{$index + 1}} name was {{player.previousName}}.</h3>
  </div>
```

You can view the example either online at http://plnkr.co/edit/ Z2faLKy0e0PF7Lx9liEW or in the Example11 folder from the source code for this chapter.

# The ngInclude directive

The ngRepeat directive example is very useful when we need to manipulate the HTML for a specific application view. However, I can easily imagine scenarios where the HTML for a player has to be reused between different views. If there is a single player game, we want to see only one player editing form rather than two. AngularJS offers a simple but powerful solution through the ngInclude directive. This directive allows the referencing of a separate file that will be loaded and rendered in the current HTML view by AngularJS.

To introduce this directive, I had to change the HTML for the ngRepeat example and add a new file that contains the player HTML markup. The following code is the new HTML for the original body element:

```
<body ng-controller="ExampleController">
  <h1>Game setup</h1>
  <div ng-repeat="player in players" ng-init="playerIndex = $index">
    <ng-include src="'player.html'"></ng-include>
  </div>
</body>
```

The following code represents the new player.html file:

```
<h2>Player {{playerIndex + 1}}</h2>
<label>Name:</label>
<input type="text" placeholder="Please enter player {{playerIndex
+ 1}} name" ng-model="player.name" ng-
focus="player.onNameFocused()">
<h3 ng-show="player.name">Player {{playerIndex + 1}} name is
{{player.name}}.</h3>
<h3 ng-show="player.previousName">Previous Player {{playerIndex +
1}} name was {{player.previousName}}.</h3>
```

You can view the example either online at http://plnkr.co/edit/ phaxRDtE8CM2EMdzc83L or in the Example12 folder from the source code for this chapter.

The first highlighted attribute is a new directive, ngInit, that evaluates an arbitrary expression. Although this directive can be used anywhere, it is best practice to only use it in the context of the ngRepeat directive. We use it to create a new scope property that is an alias of the $index variable from the ngRepeat directive. The reason behind this alias is to allow the reuse of the player markup in contexts where there is no enclosing ngRepeat directive.

The next highlighted element is the ngInclude directive, which fetches the referenced player.html file, renders it, and creates a new scope for it. The scope inherits the current ngRepeat iteration scope and its player and playerIndex properties. The last highlighted expression shows how the property created by ngInit is used in player markup.

# Creating a custom directive

While the ngInclude directive is powerful and simple, AngularJS provides another way to create reusable components. It allows you to create your own directive and use it just like any other built-in directive. The result is a more expressive HTML markup and a new component that can be used for more advanced data binding scenarios. A custom directive is also the only place where it is recommended to directly manipulate HTML elements. A controller or a service should not have any code that manipulates the DOM; this kind of code belongs to a directive.

I will start first by simplifying the previous example. The script section has a simpler service, with the playerIndex variable moved to a new property of the player object. The player.html file has some markup removed, and it will rely only on the properties of the player object.

The following code is the new main file listing for the body element:

```
<body ng-controller="ExampleController">
  <h1>Game setup</h1>
  <div ng-repeat="player in players">
    <my-player />
  </div>
  <script>
  (function() {
    "use strict";
    var myAppModule = angular.module('myApp', []);
    myAppModule.factory('playerService', function() {
      var playerIndex = 0;
      return {
        createPlayer: function() {
          playerIndex += 1;
          return {
            id: playerIndex,
```

```
                    name: "Player" + playerIndex
                };
            }
        };
    });
    myAppModule.controller('ExampleController', ['$scope',
'playerService',
        function($scope, playerService) {
            $scope.players = [playerService.createPlayer(),
playerService.createPlayer()];
        }
    ]);
    myAppModule.directive('myPlayer', function() {
        return {
            restrict: 'E',
            templateUrl: 'player.html'
        };
    });
  }());
</script>
</body>
```

The following code represents the updated `player.html` file:

```
<h2>Player {{player.id}}</h2>
<label>Name:</label>
<input type="text" placeholder="Please enter player {{player.id}}
name" ng-model="player.name">
<h3 ng-show="player.name">Player {{player.id}} name is
{{player.name}}.</h3>
```

You can view the example either online at `http://plnkr.co/edit/`
`1Kcu3MZDeKGrV7ITRUZT` or in the `Example13` folder from the source
code for this chapter.

The first highlighted element is the new custom directive, and you can view its
definition at the end of the `script` section in the last highlighted snippet. The
directive definition is a factory function that, in this scenario, returns an object with
specific properties, such as `restrict` and `templateUrl`. The `restrict` property
value ensures that the directive is applied only to HTML elements. It can take other
values such as A to match an attribute name or C to match a CSS class name, or it can
take a combination such as AE. If we don't set the property, it will take the default
value, A. The `templateUrl` property provides the link to the HTML markup that will
be rendered for the directive. The directive name follows the convention mentioned
a while ago, where the camel case directive name becomes a hyphenated directive
name in the HTML markup.

This directive does not create a scope and uses the parent scope provided by the ngRepeat directive. However, you might have a situation where you don't want to give the custom directive unrestricted access to the parent scope. In this case, you can ensure that the directive creates an isolated scope that will need to explicitly be initialized with a parent scope property. The custom directive definition is now as shown in the following code:

```
myAppModule.directive('myPlayer', function() {
      return {
        restrict: 'E',
        templateUrl: 'player.html',
        scope: {
          player: "=data"
        }
      };
    });
```

The body element content has been changed to the following code:

```
<h1>Game setup</h1>
  <div ng-repeat="currentPlayer in players">
    <my-player data="currentPlayer"/>
  </div>
```

You can view the example either online at http://plnkr.co/edit/ gUanL3Fooh8EDzh5ZfWY or in the Example14 folder from the source code for this chapter.

The directive definition has a new property, scope, in the first highlighted section. Since the property value is an object literal, it creates an isolated scope that defines data bindings between the directive scope properties and directive attributes. The last highlighted snippet shows how the player directive scope property is mapped through the data directive attribute value to the ngRepeat scope property, currentPlayer.

The = value from the directive scope definition means that the data binding is a two-way binding, and data changes will be propagated between the directive scope and parent scope. To set up one way data binding between the parent scope and directive scope, you need to replace = with @, and to bind to a parent scope function, you need to use the & symbol. In addition, if the directive attribute name needs to be the same as the directive scope property, the scope definition will turn out like the following code:

```
scope: {
    player: "="
}
```

The new directive markup needs to be changed to the following line of code:

```
<my-player player="currentPlayer"/>
```

You can view the example either online at http://plnkr.co/edit/
xPSGH92fhmTHaZS5HkcT or in the Example15 folder from the source
code for this chapter.

The examples showcased here introduce a simpler way to create custom directives
that are more powerful than ngInclude.

> There is a lot more to explore about custom directives, especially
> about manipulating DOM elements, but it is beyond the scope of
> this book. You can find more information on creating directives
> at http://code.angularjs.org/1.2.15/docs/guide/
> directive.

# Filters

Other significant components of AngularJS are filters that allow us to format an
AngularJS expression in the HTML markup in a declarative way. I have altered the
first AngularJS example to use two built-in filters, as shown in the following code:

```
<body ng-controller="ExampleController">
  <h1>Introduction</h1>
  <label>My name:</label>
  <input type="text" placeholder="Please enter name" ng-
model="name">
  <h3 ng-show="name">Hello! My name is {{name | uppercase}} and
today is {{today | date:'EEEE'}}.</h3>
  <script>
  var myAppModule = angular.module('myApp', []);
  myAppModule.controller('ExampleController', function ($scope) {
    $scope.name = "Alex Pop";
    $scope.today = new Date();
  });
  console.log(myAppModule.name);
</script>
</body>
```

You can view the example either online at http://plnkr.co/edit/
BDPGluxbcNtVpdCNbyil or in the Example16 folder from the source
code for this chapter.

Filters are applied to expressions using the | symbol, also known as the pipe operator. The first highlighted filter converts any string character from the left-hand expression to its uppercase value. The second highlighted filter formats an expression that is a date value to a specific display. We chose the day of the week here, but there are a lot of other date formats available.

You can also call the filters in the code as shown in the next example:

```
<body ng-controller="ExampleController">
  <h1>Introduction</h1>
  <label>My name:</label>
  <input type="text" placeholder="Please enter name" ng-
model="name">
  <h3 ng-show="name">Hello! My name is {{getNameWithFilter()}} and
today is {{today}}.</h3>
  <script>
  var myAppModule = angular.module('myApp', []);
  myAppModule.controller('ExampleController', function ($scope,
$filter) {
      $scope.name = "Alex Pop";
      $scope.getNameWithFilter = function(){
        return $filter('uppercase')($scope.name);
      };
      $scope.today = $filter('date')(new Date(),'EEEE');
  });
  console.log(myAppModule.name);
</script>
</body>
```

You can view the example either online at http://plnkr.co/edit/ mb11KyG9Q1tDmDVHiYwp or in the Example17 folder from the source code for this chapter. Note that we had to inject the $filter service as a dependency to be able to directly use the filter in the controller.

There are other built-in filters that can be explored at http://code.angularjs. org/1.2.15/docs/api/ng/filter, and you can also create your own custom filters. The following code snippet shows the method that the application module provides to define a custom filter:

```
<body ng-controller="ExampleController">
  <h1>Introduction</h1>
  <label>My name:</label>
  <input type="text" placeholder="Please enter name" ng-
model="name">
```

```
<h3 ng-show="name">Hello! My name is {{name | customname}}.<h3>
<script>
var myAppModule = angular.module('myApp', []);
myAppModule.filter('customname', function () {
  return function(name) {
    name = name || '';
    var customName = "";
    for (var i = 0; i < name.length; i++) {
      if(name.charAt(i) == "e") {
        customName += "3";
      }
      else if(name.charAt(i) == "o") {
        customName += "0";
      }
      else {
        customName += name.charAt(i);
      }
    }
    return customName;
  };
});
myAppModule.controller('ExampleController', function ($scope) {
  $scope.name = "Alex Pop";
});
console.log(myAppModule.name);
</script>
</body>
```

You can view the example either online at http://plnkr.co/edit/
KPrHjnui6t65XqxWVNQE or in the Example18 folder from the source code for this
chapter. The first highlighted snippet is the new filter used in the HTML markup.
The next highlighted snippet is the filter definition; it returns a function that will
convert a string value to a new value, where characters such as e and o are replaced
with numbers.

# Summary

This chapter introduced us to the fundamentals of AngularJS using a series of evolving examples for core concepts such as scopes, directives, data binding, and controllers. We then explored the AngularJS architecture, followed by topics such as JavaScript patterns, dependency injection, and services. The chapter ended with a presentation on directives and filters.

In the next chapter, we will explore the steps required to build AngularJS applications in Visual Studio.

# 2
# Creating an AngularJS Client-side Application in Visual Studio

In the previous chapter, we were introduced to the core concepts of AngularJS and components such as modules, controllers, services, directives, and filters.

In this chapter, we will learn how to use Visual Studio to build an AngularJS application, and the main sample application for this book will be initiated. We will explore the following topics here:

- Creating an AngularJS project in Visual Studio and using NuGet Package Manager
- Essential Visual Studio extensions
- Prototyping client-side components
- Organizing client-side code
- Integrating AngularJS with other JavaScript libraries and frameworks
- Routing
- Creating the client-side version of a sample bicycle rental management application

The official AngularJS documentation and examples use a command-line-based approach that leverages Node.js for tooling and to manage file dependencies. Node.js is a server-side, JavaScript software platform with a rich package ecosystem used to build high-throughput network applications. Visual Studio has support for Node.js through the "Node.js Tools for Visual Studio" project, but this book will use .NET web development features and tools instead to build AngularJS applications. This approach will ensure maximum compatibility with existing .NET projects. We will use Node.js with the AngularJS testing infrastructure, and this topic will be discussed in *Chapter 5, Testing and Debugging AngularJS Applications*.

This chapter assumes that you already know the fundamentals of .NET web development using Visual Studio.

The recommended release of Visual Studio used with the examples in this book is Visual Studio Professional 2013 Update 2 or higher. All of the examples from this book can also be built and executed with the free Visual Studio Express 2013 for Web version that is available at `www.microsoft.com/en-gb/download/details.aspx?id=40747` (with Update 2 available at `www.microsoft.com/en-us/download/details.aspx?id=42666`). This version will not allow you to install all of the Visual Studio extensions mentioned in this chapter, with the exception of Web Essentials 2013.

All of the examples in this chapter only support modern browsers, such as Google Chrome, Mozilla Firefox, and Internet Explorer 10 and higher, as they use various HTML5 features. Support for older browsers such as Internet Explorer 8 and 9 will be discussed in *Chapter 5, Testing and Debugging AngularJS Applications*.

The examples from this chapter can also be found hosted as source control repositories online. Examples 1 to 7 can be found at `http://github.com/popalexandruvasile/angularjs-dotnet-book/tree/master/Chapter2`, and examples 8 to 13 can be found at `http://github.com/popalexandruvasile/rentthatbike` as branches of the main repository (`chapter2-example8` to `chapter2-example13`).

# Using Visual Studio with NuGet to manage AngularJS and related libraries

Visual Studio 2013 has introduced a new and simpler way to create web development projects. It is now possible to create an empty web application that does not have to choose a web framework right from the beginning. The following screenshot shows the new web project dialog box:

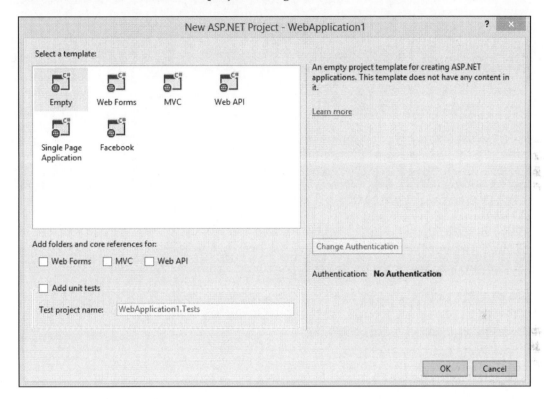

We will use this dialog box to create a new web project that does not have any web framework selected, just like in the previous screenshot. Next, we will include the two files of the last directive example (`Example18`) from *Chapter 1, Introducing AngularJS*, in this project. The project file structure should look as shown in the following screenshot:

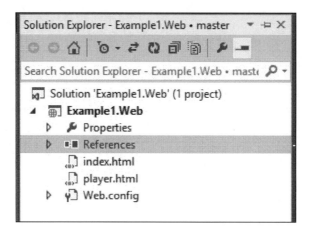

The content of the `Web.config` file contains only the minimum required configuration, which is in contrast with previous Visual Studio releases, as shown in the following code:

```
<configuration>
  <system.web>
    <compilation debug="true" targetFramework="4.5" />
    <httpRuntime targetFramework="4.5" />
  </system.web>
</configuration>
```

You can find this project in the `Example1` folder from the source code for this chapter. When you run the project by pressing *F5* or navigating to **DEBUG | Start Debugging** in Visual Studio, the web address `http://localhost:61803/index.html` will be loaded in the default browser, and it will display the example with its functionality intact.

Although we will discuss debugging in detail in *Chapter 5, Testing and Debugging AngularJS Applications*, it is worth mentioning that if you are using Visual Studio Professional with Internet Explorer as the default browser, you can easily debug the AngularJS examples from this chapter. When you set up a breaking point in any script section from an HTML file or in any JavaScript file and execute the project using the **Debug** configuration, you should be able to inspect any JavaScript object, like the one from the next screenshot:

```
master • Example1.Web (Debug|Any CPU) (Debugging) - Microsoft Visual Studio

   Continue      Debug

index.html  + X  Web.config

          var myAppModule = angular.module('myApp', []);
          myAppModule.factory('playerService', function () {
              var playerIndex = 0;
              return {
                  createPlayer: function () {
                      playerIndex += 1;
                      return {
                          id: playerIndex,
                          name: "Player" + playerIndex
                      };
                  }
              };
          });
          myAppModule.controller('ExampleController', ['$scope', 'playerService',
              function ($scope, playerService) {
                  $scope.players = [playerService.createPlayer(), playerService.createPlayer()];
              }
          ]);
          myAppModule.directive                            unction () {
              return {
                  restrict: 'E',                      __proto__    {...}
                  templateUrl: 'player.html',         id           2
                  scope: {                            name     -  "Player2"
                      player: "="
                  }
              };
          });
      }());
    </script>
  </body>
</html>
```

This is a fast and convenient way to debug JavaScript code from Visual Studio, but this feature is only available for the Internet Explorer browser, and the alternative is to use Google Chrome Developer Tools, which will be explored in *Chapter 5*, *Testing and Debugging AngularJS Applications*.

We established an easy process to create and run AngularJS applications using a minimal and unobtrusive web application project. We started a workflow that will allow us to start small and gradually incorporate additional features, libraries, and frameworks for both the client side and server side.

# Introducing NuGet

The file index.html from the previous example still has a script reference to an external AngularJS library link. It is good practice to work with local script files first and use externally hosted versions when the application is deployed in production or only when required. To add a reference to a local version of the AngularJS library, we need to use the NuGet Package Manager from Visual Studio.

NuGet is primarily a command-line tool that provides access to an online repository of software packages that can be added to a Visual Studio project. These NuGet packages will be installed in the `packages` folder within the project solution folder. Every project that is using NuGet packages will contain a `packages.config` file that will contain references to the package names and versions that are included in the current project. You can browse and search available NuGet packages at `www.nuget.org` or using the Visual Studio NuGet dialogs. The Visual Studio NuGet dialogs can be found in **Solution Explorer** in the context menu for the solution node or project nodes. For the solution node, there is a **Manage NuGet Packages for Solution...** menu, and for the project node, there is a similar menu called **Manage NuGet Packages....** Throughout this book, the NuGet command line has been used, which is available from the Visual Studio main menu under **Tools | NuGet Package Manager | Package Manager Console**. The NuGet command line has a series of built-in commands available, and the one we use to install packages is `Install-Package`. This is how you install a specific package in a Visual Studio project using NuGet Package Manager Console. This is shown in the following screenshot:

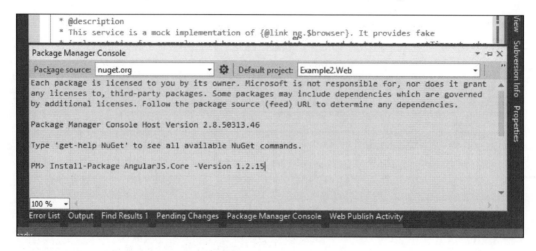

Note the dropdown that contains the project list, where you can change the project target for the current NuGet command.

Going back to the previous example, we will add a NuGet package called AngularJS. Core that contains the minimum required AngularJS files for the project. We need to run the following command in NuGet Package Manager Console:

```
Install-Package AngularJS.Core -Version 1.2.15
```

Note the package version that is specified at the end of the command. This will prevent the installation of the package using the default option, which will get the latest stable version. I will use specific versions of NuGet packages throughout this book where relevant, to ensure that you can run the examples with the same package versions that were used when the book was written.

Running the preceding command created a `scripts` folder with the AngularJS files that we need, and we can now modify the `index.html` file to replace the external AngularJS reference with a local file reference, as shown in the following code:

```
<script src="scripts/angular.js"></script>
```

You can find this example in the `Example2` folder from the source code for this chapter. When you run the example, the functionality remains unchanged; however, all of the library dependencies are now local files, and they are managed by NuGet. The next time you want to update AngularJS to a newer version, you just need to run a similar NuGet command as follows:

```
Update-Package AngularJS.Core -Version 1.2.16
```

Your project libraries are usually up to date without you having to change any file manually. You can repeat the same approach with any other JavaScript library that needs to be referenced in the project.

To see a list of potential updates that can be applied to a specific Visual Studio project, you can run the following NuGet command:

```
Update-Package –WhatIf
```

You can now specify a package name that has been taken from the output of this command and perform a specific package update. If you remove the `WhatIf` flag from the preceding command, all of the NuGet packages from the selected project will be updated.

> You can also run NuGet outside of Visual Studio from the Windows command line using the NuGet command-line utility from `http://nuget.org/nuget.exe`. More details on this tool are available at `http://docs.nuget.org/docs/reference/command-line-reference`.

# Using Visual Studio extensions for AngularJS

We have seen how NuGet helps us manage software dependencies, but Visual Studio also has support for installing extensions. An extension adds new functionality to Visual Studio. Some extensions improve the editing and file manipulation capabilities of AngularJS. In the Visual Studio main menu, when we navigate to **Tools | Extensions | Extensions Manager**, there is a menu item that allows you to either search for new extensions or update existing ones. Not all extensions are available for Visual Studio Express editions, and you need to use Visual Studio Professional or higher to install them.

The first extension is Web Essentials 2013, which is also available for Visual Studio Express 2013 for Web and introduces numerous web development features and enhancements as follows:

- For CSS, this extension provides a font and image preview, color value validation, color format conversion, and other features

- For JavaScript, this extension provides support for JSHint (which is a tool that enforces coding guidelines and best practices), autocomplete braces, **Find All References** dialog boxes, and others

- For HTML, this extension provides an image hover preview, smart tags to extract the JavaScript from the `script` tag to file and generate an AngularJS controller from an `ng-controller` attribute, and the autocompletion and validation of AngularJS attributes

There are many other features, and you can find out more on the extension website at `http://vswebessentials.com`. With this extension installed, you can review the `index.html` file from the previous example, and you will notice that any highlighted HTML validation errors have now disappeared due to the newly provided AngularJS support. You can now use AngularJS Visual Studio Intellisense when working with HTML markup and type `ng-` to view the list of available directives, like in the following screenshot:

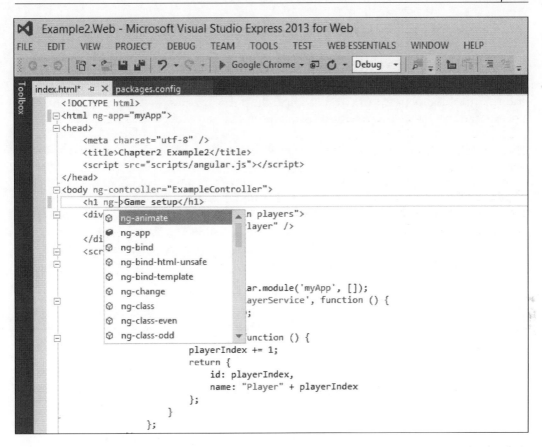

The other useful extension for AngularJS is SideWaffle Template Pack; it provides support for new project templates and new project item templates in Visual Studio Professional and higher. With this extension installed, you can now create AngularJS-specific files, such as controllers, services, directives, and modules. You can find out more about the types of projects and project items supported on the extension website at `http://sidewaffle.com`.

With these two extensions installed, Visual Studio becomes a powerful AngularJS IDE, and although the extensions are not required to build and run the examples, they are a great improvement for the Visual Studio web application development workflow.

# Prototyping client-side components

With the current setup, we have established a great starting point to explore AngularJS samples and experiment in the comfort of Visual Studio. You can easily build user interfaces with the involvement of very little JavaScript using the AngularJS directives, and you can speed up this process even more using a specialized, frontend design framework.

In the last couple of years, the rise in JavaScript frameworks has been matched by the rise in frontend design frameworks such as Bootstrap and Foundation. These frameworks provide a consistent set of HTML markup and base CSS files that will render a user interface with a specific look and feel. You can customize this look and feel by providing your own version of the base CSS or use a prebuilt one. Frontend design frameworks have a central grid system that is used to lay out and organize content. They also have support for implementing responsive web design with a lot of built-in functionality that will adapt the user interface for various screen sizes.

Visual Studio 2013 comes with built-in support for Bootstrap in any new ASP. NET Web Forms or ASP.NET MVC project, and we will use this frontend design framework to power the book's examples from now on. I will cover some of its features as they have been used in the examples, but a good place to get more in-depth documentation on them is `http://getbootstrap.com`.

The Bootstrap grid system is based on a 12-column layout that uses `div` tags and special CSS classes to differentiate between rows and columns and set column widths, offsets, and spans. We will adapt the previous example to use Bootstrap to organize the content. We need to add the NuGet package by first running the following command in NuGet Package Manager Console and then add a script reference to the base CSS file located at `Content/bootstrap.css` from the new package:

```
Install-Package bootstrap -Version 3.1.1
```

If you run the project found in the `Example3` folder from the source code for this chapter, you will see that the player content is now aligned vertically and the **Game setup** title is centered above it. If the browser width drops below 992 px, the content gets aligned horizontally to fit devices with smaller screens. The `body` element markup is now changed to the following code:

```
<div class="container">
  <div class="row">
      <div class="col-md-12 text-center">
          <h1>Game setup</h1>
      </div>
      <div class="row">
          <div class="col-md-6">
              <my-player player="players[0]" />
          </div>
          <div class="col-md-6">
              <my-player player="players[1]" />
          </div>
      </div>
  </div>
</div>
```

The Bootstrap-specific classes are highlighted in the preceding code, and the `container` class marks the layout grid. The `row` class defines grid rows, and the `col-md-6` class defines a cell that spans six grid columns. The `md` part means that the column will be aligned horizontally when displayed on medium devices with a resolution greater than or equal to 992 px, as shown in the following screenshot:

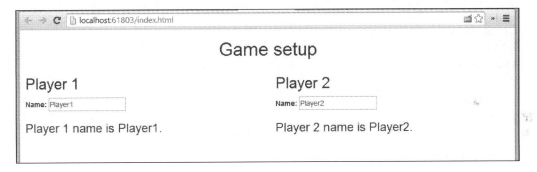

When the resolution is smaller than 992 px, the columns will collapse (the **Player 1** markup will be rendered above the **Player 2** markup). The `player.html` file uses the same Bootstrap grid system to align its controls.

> You can use the Google Chrome Windows Resizer extension available at `http://chrome.google.com/webstore/detail/window-resizer/kkelicaakdanhinjdeammmilcgefonfh` to test different browser dimensions.

With a project setup with AngularJS and Bootstrap in Visual Studio, you can now follow a more productive web application development workflow. You can prototype the user interface first with AngularJS directives and Bootstrap components, and then use JavaScript objects to populate the required data. Bootstrap will lend the application a polished look and feel, and AngularJS will make it easy to add dynamic behavior where needed, using a very expressive markup. You only need to add the server-side code to support the user interface after the user interface features and behavior have been pretty well established. Using this approach, you can easily create prototypes to test different interface designs without having to implement any server-side code to support them. This approach also allows different developers to create the user interface design in parallel with the server-side implementation.

This chapter will follow this workflow to build the main book example, and it will stop right before the implementation of the server-side code.

# Organizing client-side code

All of the examples up to this point have used a code organization that allowed you, wherever possible, to view the HTML and JavaScript in the same file. We will gradually change the next examples to be more in line with how a production-ready application code structure looks. It is time to discuss the organization of AngularJS code.

AngularJS has a starter project called angular-seed available at `http://github.com/angular/angular-seed`. The project proposes the splitting of application-specific JavaScript code into separate files, as follows:

- An `app.js` file that contains the application module definition and any code related to the application module `config` and `run` phases

- A separate file for each type of AngularJS component: a `controllers.js` file for controllers, a `services.js` for services, and other files that use the same naming convention

This organization is good when you have just a couple of AngularJS components of each type. I adapted the previous example and created a new one that uses the angular-seed project organization in the project found in the Example4 folder from the source code for this chapter. I created an app folder under scripts/app, where all of the application JavaScript now resides, and modified the index.html page to have links to the JavaScript files, replacing the previous script element. I used a single shared application module rather than a separate module for each type of AngularJS component, like in the angular-seed project. This is a more practical approach, as you usually split the code into different modules when you want to reuse the code in multiple AngularJS applications or when you require a customizable module configuration.

When you have more than a couple of components, there is a different way of organizing your code; you create a folder for each AngularJS component, such as controllers, and have a separate file for each component in that folder. All of the HTML files apart from the one that represents the entry point in the application reside in the views folder. I adapted the previous example to reflect the new project structure in the project found in the Example5 folder from the source code for this chapter. You can see the project structure in the following screenshot:

If your application gets reasonably large, there is another model to organize your AngularJS code. You start separating your project files into vertical slices, where components are grouped by their areas of functionality or features into separate parent folders such as `scripts/app/products`. All relevant components and HTML files are stored in the parent folder, and you usually have a folder, `shared`, under the location `scripts/app/` where you store components and HTML files that are reused between different application features.

# Integrating AngularJS with JavaScript libraries

Until now, the example projects have used AngularJS exclusively, but you will have to use other JavaScript libraries at some point. This raises the question about how well AngularJS works along with other libraries. Answering this question means discussing how HTML gets updated to reflect scope change.

When all of the JavaScript files have been loaded and the AngularJS application has effectively started, the application modules are configured and executed. The HTML then gets compiled by AngularJS, and the directives and controllers are associated with DOM elements. A two-way communication system is established between the scope and the DOM, where any changes get propagated from the scope to the DOM and from the DOM to the scope. External library calls or browser DOM / API calls from any AngularJS component will have to be carefully considered to identify whether it affects the AngularJS application views or scopes. Furthermore, we have the following two types of library calls that need special attention:

- An asynchronous call that will return data that needs to be assigned to a scope, such as an external library call, an XHR call, or a `window.setTimeout()` call

- A DOM manipulation call that will attempt to modify HTML elements, such as a jQuery plugin or a jQuery function

# Native JavaScript libraries and AngularJS

The first type of non-AngularJS library call needs to be changed so it calls an AngularJS service instead, where possible. You should use the built-in `$timeout` service rather than `window.setTimeout` or the `$http` service rather than an XHR call such as `jQuery.ajax()`. For operations that don't have an equivalent AngularJS service, you can directly call the special scope method, `scope.$apply()`, which was briefly mentioned in *Chapter 1, Introducing AngularJS*, as the mechanism for dirty checking. Before discussing the example for this section, we need to explore the digest cycle in AngularJS.

The built-in directives and services of AngularJS will propagate any model changes that occur outside of the AngularJS execution context by calling `scope.$apply()` and, indirectly, `scope.$digest()`. Within `scope.$digest()`, the model changes for the expressions affected by these changes will be propagated to all of the listeners registered through `scope.$watch`. The listeners are able to also perform further model changes that might trigger other listeners, and the `scope.$digest()` call ends when all of the listeners have been processed.

This constitutes the digest cycle, and it happens automatically for regular AngularJS code. When working with non-AngularJS code, you need to ensure that any scope property change that happens outside of the AngularJS execution context has a matching `scope.$apply()` method call to trigger the digest cycle. For the next example, we will use the native `window.setTimeout` method as a good example of when we need to call `scope.$apply()`.

I adapted the previous example to delay the creation of the two `player` objects using a `window.setTimeout` call, a `$timeout` call, and a `$scope.$apply()` call within the `window.setTimeout` callback. The players markup will be displayed when the expression `players.length > 0` is evaluated as true, and a message, **Creating players ...**, will be displayed when the player loading call is initiated. Although the `window.setTimeout` call is successful, the markup remains unchanged, and it only gets updated when the other two alternative calls are used. You can explore this example in the project found in the `Example6` folder from the source code for this chapter.

Most third-party, JavaScript utility libraries are compatible with AngularJS, and any JavaScript code that does not use browser-native features or tries to access the DOM should also be safe to use with AngularJS.

# Third-party user interface libraries and AngularJS

Addressing the second type of non-AngularJS library call that manipulates the DOM usually requires the creation of a new directive, where any jQuery element references need to be replaced with `angular.element()` calls. AngularJS has a built-in, jQuery-like library called jqLite, but it will use jQuery instead, if it is referenced as a script in your application. Any call to `angular.element()` will be translated as a jQLite/jQuery call. There are a couple of jQuery components that have been converted to AngularJS by the open source development community and a couple of commercial user interface libraries that are compatible with AngularJS.

AngularUI is hosted at `http://angular-ui.github.io` and is one of the better known AngularJS companion libraries. It has several AngularJS modules, such as UI.Utils and UI Bootstrap, that can be used independently from one another. The UI.Utils module provides directives such as jQuery Passthrough. This directive allows the use of jQuery functions or plugins directly in AngularJS, without having to create a new directive.

UI Bootstrap is one of the most popular AngularJS third-party modules as it provides the functionality for the Bootstrap frontend design framework from the original JavaScript files. It has directives that support the creation of modal windows, accordions, carousels, and tooltip components, to name just a few. UI Bootstrap has an alternative in the AngularStrap library that can be found at `http://mgcrea.github.io/angular-strap`.

There are also commercial libraries that provide widgets compatible with AngularJS, usually through an integration library. I'll mention Wijmo and Kendo UI as two such libraries, but there are others that are also available. They both have a subset of components that are freely available.

# Routing

One of the most distinctive features of a single-page application is client-side-based navigation between different views. If the browser switches between different application URLs, the current view should be updated seamlessly without a page request being sent from the server. AngularJS has built-in support for this feature, which is also known as routing. There are two types of routing: one based on hashbang URLs such as `www.myapp.com#/products` and `www.myapp.com#/customers` and one based on the HTML5 History API with URLs such as `www.myapp.com/products` and `www.myapp.com/customers`. For browsers that don't support the HTML5 History API, the routing will fall back to using hashbang URLs.

To set up routing in AngularJS, you have to use a separate module called ngRoute. To integrate the module package, you need to run the following command in NuGet Package Manager Console and add a reference to the scripts/angular-route.js location:

```
Install-Package AngularJS.Route -Version 1.2.15
```

The application module needs to reference the ngRoute module in its definition as shown in the following code:

```
var myAppModule = angular.module('myApp', ['ngRoute']);
```

I modified the previous example and added the routing support. The next step is to split the application into multiple views and configure the routes that will match the views. I changed the functionality of the example, and the application will now set up two types of games: a one-player game and a two-player game. I created two separate HTML files: one for a multiplayer view found in scripts/app/views/multiPlayer.html (which contains the existing players markup) and one for a single player view found in scripts/app/views/singlePlayer.html (which contains new markup for one player). The index.html file has a new directive, ngView, that replaces the original players markup. This directive will render the view that matches the current route, and you can have only one in an AngularJS application. The last step is to configure the routes in the application module config section by setting them up with the $routeProvider component, as shown in the following code:

```
myAppModule.config([
    '$routeProvider', function ($routeProvider) {
        $routeProvider
            .when('/singleplayer', { templateUrl:
'scripts/app/views/singlePlayer.html' })
            .when('/multiplayer', { templateUrl:
'scripts/app/views/multiPlayer.html' });
    }
]);
```

I am using the default routing type based on hashbang URLs, but the routes have been specified in the code using the syntax based on the HTML5 History API. This is a convention that helps us uniquely identify a route, without worrying about whether the current browser supports the HTML5 History API or not.

The changes are now complete; if we run the web project that has its default web address set to http://localhost:61803 and then navigate to http://localhost:61803/#/singleplayer, we see the markup of the editing details for one player. If we navigate to http://localhost:61803/#/multiplayer, the editing details for two players are displayed instead.

You can explore this example in the project found in the `Example7` folder from the source code for this chapter. For convenience, I also added an application menu and organized the layout of the views using Bootstrap components.

> You can also use an alternative module called AngularUI Router instead of `ngRoute`. This module uses a state machine model to define more powerful AngularJS navigation, such as multiple views per route (`ngRoute` only allows one view per route). You can find more details at `http://github.com/angular-ui/ui-router`.

# Creating a bicycle rental management application

It is now time to put all of the pieces together and create an AngularJS application that is more complex than the individual examples we have explored so far. A bicycle rental management application is a good project to build for this book, and we will start with the initial functionality covered by simple user stories. A user story is a software requirement written from the point of view of an application user that follows a constrained format: "As a (user role) I want (feature/goal) so that (I have this benefit/specific outcome)". The words between the brackets are replaced with requirements specific to your application.

For the bicycle rental management application, we only envisage a single user role at the moment: the admin user, that is, the shop assistant who is tasked with managing bicycle rental requests that have been issued by phone or e-mail. The user stories are as follows:

- As an admin user, I want to add bicycles and edit their names, types, stock quantities, and daily rent prices so that I can give details about a specific bicycle to the customers

- As an admin user, I want to introduce customer details so that I can contact customers if they have not returned a bicycle on time

- As an admin user, I want to record bicycle rental requests so that I can confirm with the customers that the bicycle they requested is booked for them

- As an admin user, I want to record bicycle rental requests for bicycles that are available in stock so that I will not be able to book a bicycle that has been rented to a different customer

These user stories are the minimum that are required to start working on the application, and they represent just the starting point of a conversation. If they had been real requirements, I would expect further refinement of the feature specifications, followed by new user stories.

We will start the application by setting up the project structure and NuGet packages as in the previous example. We will then implement the main application menu using the Bootstrap navbar component. Since this component has a special style for the application name, now is a good time to choose one, and I can think of nothing better than: Rent That Bike!

# Creating the application layout

The main menu for our application will contain three links to the three main views: **Rentals**, **Customers**, and **Bicycles**. This menu should be responsive and adapt to smaller screen sizes because we used the navbar component and kept the recommended markup. However, if you resize the browser to a width of under 768 px, you will notice that the menu collapses and that this does not have any effect on the button that should display it again. The functionality required for this resides in a Bootstrap JavaScript file called `collapse.js`, which does not work with AngularJS in its current form. Furthermore, this is where the AngularUI `UI.Bootstrap` module comes to the rescue. To install it in the project, we need to run the following command in NuGet Package Manager Console and add a reference to the `scripts/ui-bootstrap-tpls-0.10.0.js` location in `index.html`:

```
Install-Package Angular.UI.Bootstrap -Version 0.10.1
```

Next, we need to add the `ui.bootstrap` module as a dependency to our application module, and then we can start using the new provided functionality. The following code shows how the `app.js` content looks now:

```
var myAppModule = angular.module('myApp', ['ngRoute',
'ui.bootstrap']);
myAppModule.config([
  '$routeProvider', function ($routeProvider) {
    $routeProvider
        .when('/', { templateUrl:
'scripts/app/views/default.html' })
        .when('/bicycles', { templateUrl:
'scripts/app/views/bicyclesIndex.html' })
        .when('/customers', { templateUrl:
'scripts/app/views/customersIndex.html' })
        .when('/rentals', { templateUrl:
'scripts/app/views/rentalsIndex.html' });
  }
]);
```

You can explore this example in the project found in the Example8 folder from the source code for this chapter.

To make the application menu collapsible, you have to use the UI.Bootstrap collapse directive that has to be bound to a Boolean scope property that will record the current menu's collapsed state. I created an isMainMenuCollapsed scope property with a default value of false; this means that when the browser width is lower than 768 px, the menu will be visible by default. The following code is the new application menu markup, where I highlighted the changes required to make it compatible with AngularJS:

```
<nav class="navbar navbar-inverse" role="navigation">
  <div class="container-fluid">
      <div class="navbar-header">
          <button type="button" class="navbar-toggle" ng-
click="isMainMenuCollapsed = !isMainMenuCollapsed">
              <span class="sr-only">Toggle navigation</span>
              <span class="icon-bar"></span>
              <span class="icon-bar"></span>
              <span class="icon-bar"></span>
          </button>
          <a class="navbar-brand" href="#">Rent That Bike!</a>
      </div>
      <div class="collapse navbar-collapse"
collapse="isMainMenuCollapsed">
          <ul class="nav navbar-nav">
              <li><a href="#/rentals">Rentals</a></li>
              <li><a href="#/customers">Customers</a></li>
              <li><a href="#/bicycles">Bicycles</a></li>
          </ul>
      </div>
  </div>
</nav>
```

I added a separate view that only contains the view title for each application menu link. There is an additional default.html view that will greet the user each time the application starts or the application name link is clicked in the main menu. This view has a marketing message that has been built using the Bootstrap Jumbotron component.

The application HTML layout uses HTML5-specific tags to differentiate between the main application sections. The header element contains the application menu, and the section element contains a Bootstrap grid, where the application views will render as single or multiple grid rows depending on their layout needs.

We have now created the skeleton of a responsive application, which you can easily build upon and expand. At this point, we are all set to start implementing the first user story.

# Implementing the Bicycles views

The **Bicycles** view should contain a listing that displays the current stock, and it should be the starting point to add and modify a bicycle. I usually prototype the user interface first before I add complex functionality. A quick way to do this is by creating a scope property that contains an array of bicycle objects. We will populate the array with a bicycle object, and we will build the user interface next, to get a better impression of how the rendered view looks.

Next, we will create the following separate views:

- An index view to display all bicycles

- A new view to create a new bicycle

- An edit view to edit an existing bicycle

After these views are implemented, we need to create similar views for customers and rentals.

# The Bicycles index view

The previous example had a single controller called `ApplicationController`, and the views defined in `app.js` were not attached to any other controller. The `ngRoute` module allows you to associate a controller with a view that is suitable for the current route. I will create a `BicyclesController` controller, which will be instantiated whenever the `bicyclesIndex.html` file is rendered. The following code shows the initial definition of the `BicyclesController` controller:

```
myAppModule.controller('BicyclesController', ['$scope',
    function ($scope) {
        $scope.bicycles = [
            { id: 1, name: "Very fast bike", typeName: "Road
Bike", quantity: 5, rentPrice: 15 },
            { id: 2, name: "Very springy bike", typeName:
"Mountain Bike", quantity: 20, rentPrice: 17 },
            { id: 3, name: "Very classy bike", typeName: "Urban
Bike", quantity: 20, rentPrice: 14 },
            { id: 4, name: "Very colorful bike", typeName:
"Children Bike", quantity: 20, rentPrice: 9 }
        ];
    }
]);
```

I will use a `table` element with Bootstrap styles, which will give the rendered content striped rows and visible margins. The rows will be built using the `ngRepeat` directive, and the following code is the HTML that will replace the previous default content:

```
<table class="table table-bordered table table-striped">
  <thead>
    <tr>
      <th>#</th>
      <th>Name</th>
      <th>Type</th>
      <th>Quantity</th>
      <th>Rent price</th>
    </tr>
  </thead>
  <tbody>
    <tr ng-repeat="bicycle in bicycles">
      <td>{{bicycle.id}}</td>
      <td>{{bicycle.name}}</td>
      <td>{{bicycle.typeName}}</td>
      <td>{{bicycle.quantity}}</td>
      <td>{{bicycle.rentPrice | currency}}</td>
    </tr>
  </tbody>
</table>
```

You can explore this example in the project found in the `Example9` folder from the source code for this chapter.

The last column uses a built-in `currency` filter that formats values using the default currency symbol.

## The Bicycles new view

With the index view in place, it is time to implement the functionality to add a new bicycle. We need to add a new route with a new view and new controller in `app.js`. We can use the following code:

```
$routeProvider.when('/bicycles/new', { templateUrl:
'Scripts/app/views/bicyclesNew.html', controller:
'BicycleController' });
```

Access to the new view will be provided through an **Add new bicycle** button on the **Bicycles** index view, and through a similar button on the default application view. Before implementing the markup for the view, we have to do some refactoring first.

As we have two controllers working with bicycle objects, it is good practice to create a `bicyclesService` service that will contain all the business logic required to create, read, and update bicycles. The service does not have any access to the controllers, but it will be able to access other application services and AngularJS built-in services. The following are the methods of the service:

- `getBicycles()`: This method returns an array of bicycles, including the initial ones and any added ones
- `getBicycleTypes()`: This method returns an array of bicycle types to be used in `select` elements
- `createBicycle()`: This method creates an initial bicycle object to be populated with values by the user
- `addBicycle()`: This method adds a valid, new bicycle object to the existing list of bicycles

The controllers will be updated to declare the new service as a dependency, and the `BicyclesController` definition will now look like the following code:

```
myAppModule.controller('BicyclesController', ['$scope',
'bicyclesService',
            function ($scope, bicyclesService) {
                $scope.bicycles = bicyclesService.getBicycles();
            }
    ]);
```

This refactoring will allow us to reuse any similar code between different controllers and change the service without changing the controllers.

With all this in place, we can now implement the new view. For the HTML, we will use the styling specific to the Bootstrap form, and for form validation, we will use the built-in, AngularJS-form-related directives. This is a powerful combination, and it might seem a bit overwhelming if you look at the final HTML content. We will explore the required changes gradually, and start with the Bootstrap styles.

## Bootstrap form styles

Bootstrap expects all form elements to be placed in `div` elements with a `form-group` class. For the bicycle name editor, the initial HTML will look like the following code:

```
<div class="form-group">
    <label for="inputName" class="control-label">Name</label>
    <input type="text" class="form-control" name="inputName"
placeholder="Enter bicycle name here ..." required ng-
model="bicycle.name">
</div>
```

The `control-label` and `form-control` classes for form controls are also Bootstrap specific, and in addition to this, they will enforce a specific style with the `help-block` class depending on the state of the form validation. When the parent element contains a `has-error` class, the label text becomes red and the `inputName` element has a red border. The `has-error` class needs to be added programmatically.

I will also add a **Required** text to be displayed next to the `inputName` element when its value is empty. To align the controls horizontally and proportionally, I will employ Bootstrap grid column classes, and the previous HTML will be converted into the following code:

```
<div class="form-group">
  <label for="inputName" class="col-md-2 control-
label">Name</label>
  <div class="col-md-4">
      <input type="text" class="form-control" name="inputName"
placeholder="Enter bicycle name here ..." required ng-
model="bicycle.name">
  </div>
  <div class="col-md-2">
      <span class="help-block">Required</span>
  </div>
</div>
```

Note how the grid column classes can be added to individual form controls, reducing the number of HTML elements required to align the content. With the current markup, the **Required** text is always visible, so it is time to add some additional validation logic using AngularJS-form-related directives.

## AngularJS form validation

First of all, the `form` element itself is an AngularJS directive, such as the `input` and a elements. If this element has a `name` attribute set, it then becomes a special scope property object that will be available to other elements that share the same scope. This object is an instance of the `FormController` AngularJS type, which has some additional properties of its own that will help us implement the validation logic. The `FormController.$invalid` property will be true if any of the form controls has a validation error. We will use this property to disable the form **submit** button if the form is not valid. Our form name will be set to `bicycleForm`, so the **submit** button HTML will look like the following code:

```
<button type="submit" ng-disabled="bicycleForm.$invalid"
class="btn btn-primary">Add new bicycle</button>
```

The `form` element also supports an `ng-submit` attribute; it can be bound to a scope property function, which will be called when the form is submitted, as shown in the following code:

```
<form name="bicyleForm" role="form" class="form-horizontal"
novalidate ng-submit="submit()">
```

If the `form name` attribute is set, the associated scope property object will also contain some additional properties outside of the `FormController` properties. Any form control with the `ng-model` and `name` attributes set will be published as a form scope object nested property. These form controls are instances of the `NgModelController` type, which have properties of their own (such as `$invalid`, `$error`, or `$pristine`) that will help with form validation. The following code is the bicycle name markup with added validation:

```
<div class="form-group" ng-class="{'has-error':
bicyleForm.inputName.$invalid}">
   <label for="inputName" class="col-md-2 control-
label">Name</label>
   <div class="col-md-4">
      <input type="text" class="form-control" name="inputName"
placeholder="Enter bicycle name here ..." required ng-
model="bicycle.name">
   </div>
   <div class="col-md-2">
      <span ng-show="bicyleForm.inputName.$error.required"
class="help-block">Required</span>
   </div>
</div>
```

The `ngClass` directive will add a class name to the element `class` attribute if the `inputName` element does not have a valid value. We can use the `ngShow` directive to display the **Required** text when the `inputName` value is empty.

The rest of the form controls use similar styles and validation rules. The numeric `input` elements have a minimum value set, which will trigger a new validation error message, as shown in the following code:

```
<span ng-show="bicyleForm.inputQuantity.$error.min" class="help-
block">The value needs to be greater than 0</span>
```

The controller for the new view has very little code in contrast to the associated HTML file, as shown in the following code:

```
myAppModule.controller('BicycleController', ['$scope',
'$location', 'bicyclesService',
    function ($scope, $location, bicyclesService) {
        $scope.bicycleTypes = bicyclesService.getBicycleTypes();
        $scope.bicycle = bicyclesService.createBicycle();
        $scope.submit = function () {
            bicyclesService.addBicycle($scope.bicycle);
            $location.path('/bicycles');
        };
    }
]);
```

I used the built-in `$location` service to set the route after the new bicycle object is created and validated. It will redirect the browser to the index view that contains the added row.

The AngularJS form validation feature is one of the most impressive and lesser known features; it keeps the boilerplate validation code to a minimum with validation rules that have been created in a declarative manner.

You can explore the example for this section in the project found in the `Example10` folder from the source code for this chapter.

 More details on AngularJS forms can be found at `http://code.angularjs.org/1.2.15/docs/guide/forms`.

# The Bicycles edit view

To implement this view, we will use the index view as a starter point. We will add a new column with an Edit button that will navigate to the edit view. The HTML for this form will be almost identical to the one in the new view. The differences will be in the form title and in the addition of a disabled form control that shows the bicycle ID. We will use the same HTML file and controller, and the routing will be changed to the following code:

```
.when('/bicycles/new', { templateUrl:
'Scripts/app/views/bicyclesEditor.html', controller:
'BicycleController' });
.when('/bicycles/:bicycleId/edit', { templateUrl:
'Scripts/app/views/bicyclesEditor.html', controller:
'BicycleController' });
```

Note the :bicycleId route section, which will be made available as a property in the built-in $routeParams service. The BicycleController controller will now use this service to detect whether the form is in the create or edit mode, as shown in the following code:

```
$scope.isNew = !$routeParams.bicycleId;
```

We can now use this scope property to display a new form control in the edit mode and hide it in the create mode, as shown in the following code:

```
<div class="form-group" ng-show="!isNew">
  <label for="inputId" class="col-md-2 control-label">Id</label>
  <div class="col-md-1">
      <input type="text" class="form-control" name="inputId"
value="{{bicycle.id}}" disabled>
  </div>
</div>
```

When we navigate to the #/bicycles/4/edit application route, the following screenshot will be displayed:

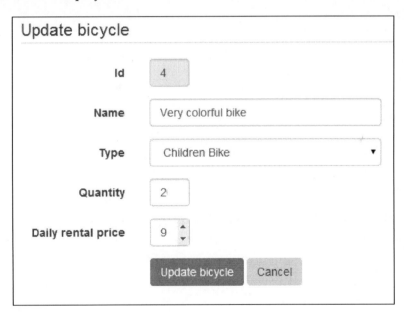

The `bicycleService` code will have an additional `getBicycle(bicyleId)` method to locate an existing bicycle by its identifier. `BicycleController` has some extra code for editing an existing bicycle object using the built-in `angular.copy()` function. When the form loads, this code will make a copy of the existing bicycle object and set it as the form model, as shown in the following code:

```
var originalBicyle = null;
if ($scope.isNew) {
  $scope.bicycle = bicyclesService.createBicycle();
  $scope.formTitle = "Add new bicycle";
} else {
  originalBicyle =
bicyclesService.getBicycle($routeParams.bicycleId);
  $scope.bicycle = angular.copy(originalBicyle);
  $scope.formTitle = "Update bicycle";
}
```

The following code will update the changes only when the form is submitted:

```
$scope.submit = function () {
  if ($scope.isNew) {
      bicyclesService.addBicycle($scope.bicycle);
  } else {
      angular.copy($scope.bicycle, originalBicyle);
      bicyclesService.updateBicycle(originalBicyle);
  }
  $location.path('/bicycles');
};
```

You can explore the example for this section in the project found in the `Example11` folder from the source code for this chapter.

# Implementing the Customers views

The next set of functionality will be implemented using a similar process with the **Bicycles** views. A customer object will have a first and last name, an e-mail ID, and a phone number. Apart from the phone number, all other properties are required. The e-mail form control will also enforce a valid e-mail format using the following markup:

```
<div class="form-group" ng-class="{'has-error':
customerForm.inputEmail.$invalid}">
  <label for="inputEmail" class="col-md-2 control-
label">Email</label>
  <div class="col-md-4">
```

```
        <input type="email" class="form-control" name="inputEmail"
placeholder="Enter email here ..." required ng-
model="customer.email">
    </div>
    <div class="col-md-2">
        <span ng-show="customerForm.inputEmail.$error.required"
class="help-block">Required</span>
        <span ng-show="customerForm.inputEmail.$error.email"
class="help-block">Not a valid email</span>
    </div>
</div>
```

When the e-mail is not in a valid format, a validation message will be displayed, and we will not have to write any JavaScript code to implement it.

You can explore the example for this section in the project found in the `Example12` folder from the source code for this chapter.

# Implementing the Rentals views

A rental object will have an initial set of properties, such as the start date, end date, bicycle, customer, quantity of bicycles rented, total rental price, and a Boolean property, which is set if the rental has been paid. I created a couple of rental objects that reference the sample data created for the previous view. I initialized the start and end dates using a popular date utility library called `moment.js`, which I added to the project using the following NuGet Package Manager command:

`Install-Package Moment.js`

Note that no version has been specified because popular JavaScript utility libraries are usually stable, safe to update, and compatible with AngularJS.

As we are now editing a range of dates, I added some business logic validation in the `rentalsService` service, which throws an exception if the start date is greater than the end date for a modified rental. AngularJS will employ the `$exceptionHandler` service to log all exceptions to the browser JavaScript console. I had to change this default behavior and use a built-in service decorator component in the `app.js` file, as shown in the following code:

```
myAppModule.config(['$provide', function ($provide) {
  $provide.decorator('$exceptionHandler', ['$delegate', function
($delegate) {
      return function (exception, cause) {
          $delegate(exception, cause);
          alert(exception.message);
      };
  }]);
}]);
```

A service decorator is an AngularJS component that can change the behavior of a service by replacing or augmenting its functionality. The previous exception helper behavior is in place, and I just added the desired functionality that will display an alert for each exception.

You might have also noticed the code related to `select` elements when a bicycle or customer is changed. There are separate properties, `bicycleId` and `customerId`, that are bound to the current selected item key. The associated bicycle and customer objects are updated only when needed: before the changes are submitted or when a related property needs to be updated when the selection has changed.

You can explore the example for this section in the project found in the `Example13` folder from the source code for this chapter.

With the final example from this chapter, we have reached the limitations of the JavaScript application. We need to validate the bicycle stock to ensure that we don't try to rent bicycles that are not available. Even if we implement the validation logic in JavaScript, when we need to store data persistently by calling a web service, we need to revalidate the data on the server. Any data sent to the server can be manipulated in the browser client, so it is good practice to validate data on the server even if it passes client validation.

# Summary

This chapter guided us through the workflow to create an AngularJS client-side application in Visual Studio. The first half of the chapter covered the basics of how to use Visual Studio to implement AngularJS applications. The second half covered the implementation of the client-side functionality for the main example of this book.

In the next chapter, we will take a look at the theory behind web services, followed by a practical guide to implementing web services for an AngularJS application.

# 3

# Creating .NET Web Services for AngularJS

The previous chapter covered creating AngularJS applications using a workflow based on Visual Studio, and a sample client-side application was created incrementally.

In this chapter, you will learn about RESTful web services; how to use a .NET web service framework, which is a great fit for AngularJS; and how to create web service resources for AngularJS. We will cover the following topics:

- RESTful web services
- .NET web services frameworks
- Overview of the ServiceStack web framework with examples
- Creating web services methods for the sample application
- Calling RESTful web services in AngularJS

This chapter assumes that you are familiar with the HTTP protocol, XML and JSON data formats, AJAX and building and calling web services programmatically. All the web configuration files mentioned in this chapter target IIS 7.0 and above.

The examples from this chapter can also be found hosted as source control repositories online. Examples 1 to 4 can be found at `http://github.com/ popalexandruvasile/angularjs-dotnet-book/tree/master/Chapter3`, and examples 5 to 7 can be found at `http://github.com/popalexandruvasile/ rentthatbike` as branches of the main repository (`chapter3-example5` to `chapter3-example7`).

# RESTful web services

Ever since ASP.NET was launched as part of the .NET framework in 2002, it came with built-in web services support. This feature is known as ASP.NET Web Services and it was based on the emerging **Simple Object Access Protocol (SOAP)** protocol. SOAP is primarily an XML-based web services protocol that was developed as a **World Wide Web Consortium (W3C)** standard in 1998. The protocol has an extensive specification, currently at Version 1.2, and it allows a wide range of transport methods and message formats. The SOAP protocol support was extended with **Windows Communication Foundation (WCF)** in 2006 as part of the .NET 3.0 release. WCF is a web services framework that supports all the features of the SOAP 1.2 specification and it came as a replacement for ASP.NET Web Services.

In parallel with the SOAP standardization process, Roy Fielding introduced the concept of **Representational State Transfer (REST)** in 2000 in his doctoral dissertation. REST is an architectural style for describing properties and constraints of distributed systems that use hypermedia resources. An example of such a distributed system is the **World Wide Web (WWW)**, and an example of a hypermedia resource is a web page. REST can be used to describe web services and they are called RESTful web services if they satisfy the following set of constraints defined by Roy Fielding:

- **Client-server**: There is a separation of concerns where the client is isolated from the server data-storage-specific implementation

- **Stateless**: The communication sessions between client and server don't rely on session data stored on the server

- **Cacheable**: The data received can be cached by the client if it is marked as cacheable

- **Uniform interface**: This consists of a group of four further constraints:

    ○ **Identification of resources**: The separate resources are identified uniquely

    ○ **Manipulation of resources through representations**: The resources have representations that can be used to change them without any additional data

    ○ **Self-descriptive messages**: The client has all the data required to manipulate a resource when the resource is received

    ○ **Hypermedia as the engine of application state**: A resource representation contains data about the actions or transitions that are available for that resource

- **Layered system**: The client is unaware of how many intermediary layers exist between it and the server
- **Code on demand (optional)**: The server can send code that is executed by the client and this is the only optional constraint

These constraints facilitate architectural properties like performance, scalability, simple interfaces, modifiability, visibility, portability, and reliability. A RESTful web service will easily conform to most of these constraints if it uses HTTP 1.1 as the communication protocol, URLs to identify its resources, and HTTP verbs to manipulate its resources. As a consequence of meeting these constraints, web services will benefit from the REST architectural properties without having to define a specific standard or undergo a significant implementation effort.

The constraint of **Hypermedia as the Engine of Application State (HATEOAS)** requires a more involved implementation effort on the server and client compared to other constraints. This aspect made it relatively less popular in the design of RESTful web services and this constraint will not be enforced in the web services examples of this book.

RESTful web services are an alternative to SOAP services and have gained a lot of ground in the last couple of years. They are heavily used in software-as-a-service products, mobile applications, and single-page web applications to name just a few use cases. They primarily use JSON as the data format because it is natively supported by browsers and has a smaller payload compared to XML.

AngularJS has built-in first-class support for RESTful web services frameworks with its ngResource module. AngularJS can also use data provided by any web service that returns JSON, which is a scenario that can be used for calls that are not frequent or essential. For a fully featured AngularJS application, the optimal scenario is to use dedicated RESTful web services endpoints rather than trying to retrofit legacy or generic web services frameworks like ASP.NET Web Services or WCF.

# Choosing a RESTful web services framework

Although it is possible to use WCF to build RESTful web services, it involves a significant development effort. This led to Microsoft building a separate web services framework called ASP.NET Web API to fully support RESTful web services. Because it was released in 2012 (six years after the initial WCF release), alternative frameworks built by the .NET developer community were already released and actively developed at that point in time. Frameworks like OpenRasta (`http://openrasta.org`), ServiceStack (`http://servicestack.net`), NancyFX (`http://nancyfx.org`), and Simple.Web (`http://blog.markrendle.net/2012/06/01/simple-web`) have filled the need for simpler, more productive frameworks that can be used to build RESTful web services. They were largely inspired by efforts made in other developer communities like Ruby with its Ruby on Rails and Sinatra web frameworks. These frameworks were built following best practices and open standards with a focus on developer productivity. These efforts were recognized and even emulated by Microsoft, which mentions and recommends these frameworks on the ASP.NET official website at `www.asp.net/web-api/open-source`. Microsoft, in 2012, effectively made their entire web development stack available as open source projects that anyone can contribute to or modify and reuse freely.

ASP.NET Web API is a relatively new framework compared to its .NET alternatives. Up until late 2013, when its 2.0 Version was released, it was missing significant features like **Cross-origin Resource Sharing (CORS)**. CORS allows browsers to make cross-domain calls in scenarios where the web page is trying to access web services hosted on different domains. An example is when a web page loaded from the URL `www.myapp.com/items` makes an AJAX call to load data from the URL `www.mywebservice.com/items`. CORS functionality was contributed to the ASP.NET Web API project by the developer community. JSONP (JSON with padding) is a feature that is similar to CORS and works for older browsers; it is not provided as a built-in component in ASP.NET Web API as of its 2.1 Version. Given this background and because some of the alternative frameworks can be used even with .NET 3.5, we will not use ASP.NET Web API as the preferred web services framework in this book.

# Why ServiceStack is a great fit for AngularJS

AngularJS is a rapidly evolving framework with frequent releases that requires a mature and flexible web services framework. One of its main drivers was improving developer productivity, and the web services frameworks developed by the .NET community shared the same driver when they were released. Using any one of these frameworks should bring about significant productivity improvements compared to WCF and even ASP.NET Web API.

We will use ServiceStack as the preferred web services framework throughout this book. It has a number of advantages that make it a great fit for AngularJS, as follows:

- JSONP and CORS support out of the box with an efficient and versatile built-in JSON serializer

- A message-based architecture that simplifies web service endpoint development

- Extensive support for content negotiation, caching, authentication, and authorization

Other advantages that make it a great web services framework are as follows:

- **One-stop framework**: ServiceStack is designed to be a one-stop framework and covers essential everyday development needs. It allows its parts to be replaced easily, such as the dependency injection framework, the session and security related providers. It embeds popular open source components like Funq for dependency injection, FluentValidation for implementing business rule validation, MiniProfiler for performance monitoring, and it provides its own components such as ServiceStack.Text for serialization.

- **Seamless integration**: ServiceStack integrates seamlessly with ASP.NET MVC and it can also be used on its own as an alternative to ASP.NET MVC.

- **Community involvement**: It has over 200 contributors with a very active discussion group and lot of samples. It has a rich ecosystem that extends its default set of features.

- **Maturity**: It was around for a couple of years with consistent and frequent commits from its authors and contributors.

- **Great documentation**: ServiceStack has a very well-written and thorough wiki, lots of blog entries, podcasts, and screencasts and online courses.

# ServiceStack overview

ServiceStack has two major versions available on NuGet. One is the 3.9 Version, which is a mature version with a large install base that targets .NET 3.5. The 3.9 Version has a BSD license, which is one of the most permissive licenses available. The other major version is 4.0, which targets .NET 4.0 and was released in early 2014. It is dual-licensed with an AGPL license and a commercial license with a free usage quota. Throughout this book, we will use the 3.9 Version as it does not have any licensing limitations and the effort to upgrade to the 4.0 Version should be relatively small for the features used in this book.

>  ServiceStack also supports views similar to ASP.NET MVC but explaining this functionality is outside of the scope of this book.

Before discussing ServiceStack in more detail, let's explore an example of a web service built with ServiceStack.

# Setting up the ServiceStack starter project

Firstly, we need to create a new empty ASP.NET web application project like we did in the previous chapter. Then we need to add the NuGet ServiceStack package that specifies the version used in this book; we use the following command:

```
Install-Package ServiceStack -Version 3.9.71 -DependencyVersion
Highest
```

Note that we had to use a new NuGet switch, DependencyVersion, that will ensure we install ServiceStack 3.9 dependencies with the highest version available. Next, we need to modify the web.config file to integrate ServiceStack in the ASP.NET pipeline and add this to the system.webServer configuration section using the following code:

```
<handlers>
  <add path="*" name="ServiceStack.Factory"
type="ServiceStack.WebHost.Endpoints.ServiceStackHttpHandlerFactor
y, ServiceStack" verb="*" preCondition="integratedMode"
resourceType="Unspecified" allowPathInfo="true" />
</handlers>
```

ServiceStack needs a configuration class to be created, which will have the following code:

```
public class AppHost : AppHostBase
{
   public AppHost()
        : base("Chapter3 Example1", typeof (AppHost).Assembly) {}

   public override void Configure(Funq.Container container) {}
}
```

Note that the configuration class derives from `AppHostBase`, which needs to be used when ServiceStack web services are hosted in an ASP.NET application.

 ServiceStack also supports self-hosting and the main configuration class needs to derive from `AppHostHttpListenerBase` instead of `AppHostBase` when using Version 3.9. For Version 4.0, the main configuration class should be `AppSelfHostBase`.

The class constructor specifies the service name and the list of assemblies where ServiceStack web services are present. The `AppHost.Configure` method provides access to the dependency injection infrastructure. Here, you can perform further ServiceStack configuration and inject or modify application dependencies.

The final change is to create a `Global.asax` file using the Visual Studio **New Item...** dialog and initialize the ServiceStack configuration class as shown in the following code:

```
protected void Application_Start(object sender, EventArgs e)
   {
        new AppHost().Init();
   }
```

At this point, we have a working ServiceStack application skeleton that is ready to start hosting web services. You can find the project in the `Example1` folder from the source code for this chapter. When you run it, the start address `http://localhost:54114/metadata` is loaded and you can view the built-in ServiceStack web services metadata page. At the moment, there are no web services but this will change soon.

# Creating ServiceStack web services

Let's add the first web service that will provide a list of players for the /players route and specific player data for a route such as /players/2. The example contains the web service class PlayersService together with the classes GetPlayers and GetPlayer that represent web service requests. The last class of the example, that is, Player encapsulates the data returned by the web service methods, as shown in the following code:

```
public class PlayersService : IService
{
  public List<Player> Get(GetPlayers request)
  {
      return GetPlayers();
  }

  public Player Get(GetPlayer request)
  {
      return GetPlayers().Single(p => p.Id == request.Id);
  }

  private List<Player> GetPlayers()
  {
      return new List<Player>
      {
          new Player{ Id= 1, FirstName="Angela", LastName =
"Evans"},
          new Player{ Id= 2, FirstName="Jack", LastName =
"Marshall"},
      };
  }
}

[Route("/players", "GET")]
public class GetPlayers : IReturn<List<Player>> {}

[Route("/players/{Id}", "GET")]
public class GetPlayer : IReturn<Player>
{
  public int Id { get; set; }
}
```

```
public class Player
{
  public int Id { get; set; }

  public string FirstName { get; set; }

  public string LastName { get; set; }
}
```

You can view the example in the project found in the `Example2` folder from the source code of this chapter.

The `PlayersService` class represents a web services container that can have multiple endpoints. It only needs to implement the `IService` marker interface to be processed by ServiceStack.

 A marker interface does not have any properties and methods.

The method `public List<Player> Get(GetPlayers request)` represents an actual web service method. Note that the `GetPlayers` parameter's class, which represents a web service request, has a `Route` attribute. This attribute defines the relative URL for the request and the HTTP verbs that are accepted. If you navigate to the address `http://localhost:54114/players`, you will see a page showing the list of sample players, as shown in the following screenshot:

When you navigate to a web service method in the browser, ServiceStack generates a human-readable HTML page. This page also contains links to all the formats supported by the web service method. To force the output to be JSON content, you either click on the **json** link or navigate directly to the address `http://localhost:54114/players?format=json` or `http://localhost:54114/players.json`. This is the output that a JavaScript client will receive as long as the HTTP header `Accept` is set to `application/json`. Without making any special configuration, ServiceStack provides support for the JSON, XML, and CSV formats, together with its own efficient serialization format JSV (JSON separated values).

You will notice that there is no exception handling code in this example. What happens if we misspell a route and navigate to the address `http://localhost:54114/playerss`? ServiceStack has built-in automated exception handling that will catch any unhandled exception and return a formatted response depending on the type of the error.

# Using the ServiceStack C# client

The `GetPlayers` class implements a generic interface, `IReturn<List<Player>>`. The interface allows .NET clients to infer the return type of the web service method directly from the request class. In the console application project from the `Example2` solution, you can find the following code that calls the previous web service method:

```
var client = new JsonServiceClient("http://localhost:54114/");
List<Player> players = client.Get(new GetPlayers());
```

We are using a built-in ServiceStack web service client of type `JsonServiceClient` to make the web service request. The web service client calls the generic `Get` method, which accepts an `IReturn<T>` parameter. This will infer the route to the web service method and the return type directly from the `GetPlayers` class instance. The example represents a very concise and simple way of calling a web service with .NET code. It will be especially useful when testing web services.

# The ServiceStack infrastructure

ServiceStack is built on top of the `IHttpHandler` interface and this is the only piece of ASP.NET infrastructure that it needs. ServiceStack uses established design patterns to define and implement its infrastructure, and one of these patterns is the **Data Transfer Object (DTO)**, originally defined by Martin Fowler. A DTO is an object created with the specific purpose of sending and receiving data between application layers or application boundaries. The request classes `GetPlayers` and `GetPlayer` from `Example2` are a typical implementation of a DTO.

In `Example2`, we also defined standalone classes for a service, a request, and a response that did not inherit any class representing the ServiceStack infrastructure. This underlines a core principle of the ServiceStack architecture, which is to use simple, lightweight objects for its infrastructure needs and allow developers to reuse their own data structures to the maximum possible degree.

# Routing

The `IService` interface allows ServiceStack to identify all classes that define web services when the application starts. Within a service class, ServiceStack will scan all methods with names mapping to HTTP verbs like `Get`, `Post`, `Put`, and `Delete`. It will also find methods named `Any` that match any HTTP verb. It will then look at the method parameter and will extract the information stored in the `Route` attribute.

 ServiceStack also supports a fluent API to define routes that can be optionally configured in the `AppHost.Configure` method.

ServiceStack can now build the list of operations that are available for the application. You can view them in the metadata page of the `Example2` example by following the **Operations Metadata** link (the link is only visible when the project is built in debug mode). The following screenshot shows the metadata page:

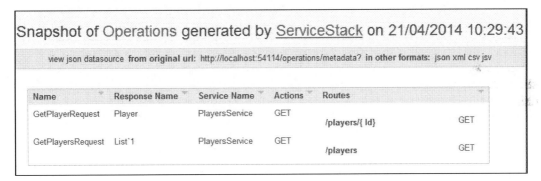

Any request received by the application will be matched against the list of operations. The request DTO will be extracted from its URL, query string, and from the body of the request regardless of its format: HTML, JSON, XML, or any other format configured for the application. If ServiceStack can create a request DTO matching a specific operation, the next step will be to apply any request filters to it.

# Request and response filters

A request filter can be configured in the `AppHost.Configure` method and is a delegate that takes the following parameters:

- `IHttpRequest`, which wraps the application host request data

- `IHttpResponse`, which wraps the application host response data

- An object instance, which is the current request DTO

The previous example is now changed to include a request filter that will prevent the application from working when using the HTTP protocol rather than HTTPS, as shown in the following code:

```
public override void Configure(Funq.Container container)
{
  RequestFilters.Add((request, response, requestDTO) =>
  {
      if(!request.IsSecureConnection)
      {
          throw new Exception("The application needs to be
secured. Use https instead of http for hosting!");
      }
  });
}
```

You can view the example in the project found in the `Example3` folder from the source code of this chapter. A similar filter is available for the service response, making the filters an efficient way to perform any operation that can be applied to all web service methods.

You can also define request and response filters as custom attributes. They can be declared in the request and response DTOs or in the service classes. More details can be found at http://github.com/ServiceStackV3/ServiceStackV3/wiki/Request-and-response-filters.

# Dependency injection

With the filters out of the way, the request DTO is now ready to be passed to the service method that matches the current route. At this point, ServiceStack has resolved all service dependencies configured in `AppHost.Configure` and will inject them in all services that require them. A service dependency is a class or interface that is declared in the service constructor or as a service public property, and will be injected by ServiceStack when the service is instantiated. This process is where we find similarities with AngularJS dependency injection and both frameworks share the same purpose as follows:

- To allow a central, flexible method to define dependencies (`AppHost. Configure` for ServiceStack and the `module.config` phase for AngularJS); this chapter will showcase this feature

- To ensure all components are testable and easy to test (more about this will be explored in *Chapter 5, Testing and Debugging AngularJS Applications*)

The previous example was modified to show how dependency injection works in ServiceStack. The `PlayersService.GetPlayers()` method was refactored to a new class, `PlayersRepository`. The `PlayersService` class was changed to the following:

```
public class PlayersService : IService
{
  public PlayersRepository Repository { get; set; }

  public List<Player> Get(GetPlayers request)
  {
      return Repository.GetPlayers();
  }

  public Player Get(GetPlayer request)
  {
      return Repository.GetPlayers().Single(p => p.Id ==
request.Id);
  }

  public Player Post(Player player)
  {
      Repository.AddPlayer(player);
      return player;
  }
}
```

Note the new property of type `PlayersRepository` that will be automatically injected by ServiceStack if we have registered it as an autowired instance in `AppHost.Configure`. By default, all auto-wired dependencies have a singleton scope: the same dependency instance will be injected everywhere it is declared. The following code is the dependency registration code:

```
public override void Configure(Funq.Container container)
    {
        container.RegisterAutoWired<PlayersRepository>();
    }
```

You can view the example in the project found in the `Example4` folder from the source code of this chapter.

## Automatic validation

ServiceStack can also apply automatic validation to the request DTO. To showcase this feature, the `Player` class was changed as follows and can now be used as a POST request with its new attribute:

```
[Route("/players", "POST")]
public class Player : IReturn<Player>
```

A new `PlayersService.Post` method was added that will add a new player object to the existing players' list. Next, a player validator class was declared as follows:

```
public class PlayerValidator : AbstractValidator<Player>
    {
        public PlayerValidator()
        {
            RuleFor(p => p.FirstName).NotEmpty();
            RuleFor(p => p.LastName).NotEmpty();
        }
    }
```

You can view the example in the project found in the same `Example4` folder from the source code of this chapter.

The validator class uses the FluentValidation library, which is included in ServiceStack. The library provides various helpers that allow for the creation of business rules for validating class properties or other complex validation scenarios. More examples of validation rules will be showcased later on in this chapter.

 You can find more information about all supported validations at `http://fluentvalidation.codeplex.com`.

Although this section is about automatic validation, you can also validate a player object manually if you instantiate the validator class and call its `Validate` method. You can reuse the validation logic between web services and other application components.

Testing POST and PUT web services requests usually requires using a tool that has a visual interface to edit the request DTO. A great web services testing tool called *Postman* is available as a Google Chrome extension at `www.getpostman.com`. The following screenshot shows the values used to test creating a new player with empty `FirstName` and `LastName` property values:

Note the request result at the bottom of the screenshot, which is a JSON-formatted validation exception. This was made possible by the automatic exception handling provided by ServiceStack.

To enable automatic validation, the `AppHost.Configure` method needs to have the following code added to it:

```
Plugins.Add(new ValidationFeature());
container.RegisterValidators(typeof(AppHost).Assembly);
```

The first line in the preceding code enables automatic validation by registering the validation plugin. ServiceStack has an extensible plugin system with many built-in plugins available. Some of these plugins, such as `ValidationFeature`, need to be registered explicitly. Other plugins are autoregistered, such as `MetadataFeature`, which enables the metadata page that was used in the examples, or `CSVFormat`, which provides support for the CSV serialization format. These plugins can be removed if required through the `AppHost.Plugins` property, as shown in the following code:

```
Plugins.RemoveAll(p => p is CsvFormat);
```

After the request DTO is validated, it is passed to the service instance, and this is where the custom application code takes over. If the request is processed successfully, the response will be returned to the client with any configured response filters applied as the final step.

So far, we have enumerated just a handful of the ServiceStack features, but this should provide a good starting point for our main application example. Some features, such as authentication and authorization, will be explored later on in the book as part of the upcoming examples.

You can find more information about the ServiceStack 3.9 Version at `http://github.com/ServiceStackV3/ServiceStackV3/wiki` or about the ServiceStack 4.0 Version at `http://github.com/ServiceStack/ServiceStack/wiki`.

# Creating web service methods for the sample application

We can now revisit the Rent That Bike! application from the previous chapter and start implementing its required web services. The first thing to do is enable the project for ServiceStack integration as detailed at the beginning of this chapter. With this in place, we set the project start-up page to `http://localhost:61803/metadata`; the basic ServiceStack integration is completed.

# ServiceStack project structure

Before we add any file, we should explore some project layout options. A typical ServiceStack implementation will include, as a minimum, service classes and request and response DTO classes. It is good practice to separate these into namespaces or even different assemblies for better maintainability for medium-sized projects. For larger projects, you could have business logic and data models that are reused between different components or applications. In this case, another good practice is to have all this logic also separated into its own namespace or assembly. We will use the ServiceStack guidance available at `http://github.com/ServiceStack/ServiceStack/wiki/Physical-project-structure` and ensure our project structure is similar by performing the following steps:

1. Create a namespace for the service classes called `RentThatBike.Web.ServiceInterface` that will contain services like `BicyclesService` and `CustomersService`.

2. Create a namespace for the request and response DTOs called `RentThatBike.Web.ServiceModel` that will also contain data model classes such as `Bicycle` and `Customer` in the nested namespace `RentThatBike.Web.ServiceModel.Types`.

If the project size grows further, the next step would be to move the `RentThatBike.Web.ServiceInterface` namespace into a separate assembly such as `RentThatBike.ServiceInterface` and even add a new assembly such as `RentThatBike.Logic` to contain classes that are reused outside of web services. This structure is just a guideline and you might choose a completely different structure depending on your application size and needs.

# Implementing Bicycles-related web services

With the basic project structure in place, we can now start implementing the `BicyclesService` class, which will contain all the web service methods related to bicycles. We start by replicating the functionality from the `bicyclesService.js` file and create a `BicycleRepository` class that will maintain the list of existing bicycles and provide methods to retrieve them. This class will be the first dependency for the `BicyclesService` class and is declared as a public property in preparation for dependency injection.

## The GET web service methods

The initial service implementation contains web service methods mapped to the GET HTTP verb and named `Get` accordingly. The service has a `BicycleRepository` property that encapsulates data access logic, as shown in the following service class:

```
public class BicyclesService : IService
{
  public BicycleRepository BicycleRepository { get; set; }

  public List<Bicycle> Get(GetBicycles request)
  {
      return BicycleRepository.GetAll().ToList();
  }

  public Bicycle Get(GetBicycle request)
  {
      return BicycleRepository.Single(b => b.Id == request.Id);
  }
}
```

You can explore the example code together with the `BicycleRepository`, `Bicycle`, and request DTOs implementations in the project found in the `Example5` folder from the source code of this chapter.

We had to register the `BicycleRepository` type as a dependency in the `AppHost.Configure` method and it will be automatically injected in the `BicyclesService` class by ServiceStack, as expected.

We have now implemented the GET web service methods and we can use the browser to request resources like `http://localhost:61803/bicycles` or `http://localhost:61803/bicycles/2`.

# The POST web service method

Recall that the new bicycle form validated the Name, Type, Quantity, and RentPrice fields. These validations have to be replicated on the server because the web service method can be called by any type of client and we cannot trust the JavaScript code fully. For this, we created a new BicycleValidator class, as follows, that contains all the expected validations plus a new one to ensure the new bicycle name is unique:

```
public class BicycleValidator: AbstractValidator<Bicycle>
{
  public BicycleValidator(BicycleRepository bicycleRepository)
  {
      RuleFor(b => b.Name).NotEmpty();
      RuleFor(b => b.Quantity).GreaterThan(0);
      RuleFor(b => b.RentPrice).GreaterThan(0);
      Custom(b =>
      {
          bool bicycleWithSameNameExists =
bicycleRepository.Get(x => x.Name.ToLower() ==
b.Name.ToLower()).Any();
          if (bicycleWithSameNameExists)
          {
              return new ValidationFailure("Name","A bicycle with
the same name already exists.", "AlreadyExists");
          }
          return null;
      });
  }
}
```

The validator has the BicycleRepository dependency declared in its constructor and this dependency is already registered in the AppHost.Configure method. Note the GreaterThan validation helper methods and the Custom method, which checks for bicycles that have the same name as the one currently being validated. The Custom method needs to create its own validation failure message rather than rely on built-in messages like the other helper methods.

To finalize the `BicyclesService.Post` web service method, we need to create the matching request DTO using the following code:

```
[Route("/bicycles", "POST")]
public class PostBicycle : IReturn<Bicycle>
{
    public Bicycle Bicycle { get; set; }
}
```

Note how we exposed a nested bicycle object property rather than a set of properties matching the individual bicycle fields. Using this approach means that the request DTO validator will delegate the actual validation to the `BicycleValidator` class we declared earlier, as shown in the following code:

```
public class PostBicycleValidator : AbstractValidator<PostBicycle>
    {
        public PostBicycleValidator(BicycleValidator
BicycleValidator)
        {
            RuleFor(r => r.Bicycle).SetValidator(BicycleValidator);
        }
    }
```

We will also have to register `BicycleValidator` in the `AppHost.Configure` method because only request and response DTO validators are automatically registered by ServiceStack. This is how the method looks after the required change:

```
public override void Configure(Container container)
{
  Plugins.Add(new ValidationFeature());
  container.RegisterValidators(typeof(AppHost).Assembly);
  container.RegisterAutoWired<BicycleRepository>();
  container.RegisterAutoWired<BicycleValidator>();
}
```

We are now ready to test the validation using the Postman web services testing tool. If we call the method using a JSON object with invalid values, the following is how the request and response will look:

The response is a JSON-formatted object that has a collection of validation errors that allows the client to build a meaningful error message if required. Because we tried to insert a bicycle with a name that is already in use, we also have a validation error for it. Passing valid values will successfully create a new bicycle object that will be visible when we request the `http://localhost:61803/bicycles` resource in the browser. Any bicycle changes are persisted between requests because the `BicycleRepository` instance is registered as a singleton dependency; that is, there is only one instance shared between all class instances that require it.

The code described previously is in the project found in the same `Example5` folder from the source code of this chapter.

# The PUT web service method

When modifying an existing bicycle, we need to ensure the `BicycleValidator` class works slightly differently. It should ensure a valid `Id` property is specified and the `Name` property does not clash with the other existing bicycles. It needs to apply different validation rules depending on if the current request is a POST or a PUT. ServiceStack provides a convenient new method signature called RuleSet that accepts an enumeration value mapped to HTTP verbs. The following code is the updated `BicycleValidator` code with validation rules that apply to POST HTTP requests:

```
RuleSet(ApplyTo.Post, () =>
    {
        RuleFor(b => b.Id).Equal(0);
        Custom(b =>
        {
            bool bicycleWithSameNameExists =
                bicycleRepository.Get(x => x.Name.ToLower() ==
b.Name.ToLower()).Any();
            if (bicycleWithSameNameExists)
            {
                return new ValidationFailure("Name", "A bicycle
with the same name already exists.", "AlreadyExists");
            }
            return null;
        });
    });
```

Note that we added a rule that enforces the `Id` property to be `0` when a new bicycle is created to prevent any issues when the object is persisted to the data store.

The following code is the validation code that applies when a PUT HTTP request is being processed:

```
RuleSet(ApplyTo.Put, () =>
{
  RuleFor(b => b.Id).GreaterThan(0);
  Custom(b =>
  {
      bool bicycleWithSameNameExists =
          bicycleRepository.Get(x => x.Name.ToLower() ==
b.Name.ToLower() && x.Id != b.Id).Any();
      if (bicycleWithSameNameExists)
      {
```

```
            return new ValidationFailure("Name", "A bicycle with the
    same name already exists.",
                "AlreadyExists");
        }
        return null;
    });
});
```

The new `void RuleSet(ApplyTo appliesTo, Action action)` method signature
that ServiceStack added to the original FluentValidation `AbstractValidator<T>`
class builds on the existing `void RuleSet(string ruleSetName, Action action)`
method signature. However, when a `RuleSet` method is present, ServiceStack will
also execute any existing `RuleFor` methods, and this functionality is different from
FluentValidation.

The request DTO validator `PutBicycleValidator` has a new validation rule added
that ensures the bicycle ID requested in the URL is the same as the one passed in the
request body. This validation rule is implemented using a predicate validator that
has the following code:

```
RuleFor(r => r.Id).Must((r,id) => id ==
r.Bicycle.Id).WithMessage("There is a mismatch between the bicycle
id from the URL and the one from the request body !");
```

The code described previously is in the project found in the `Example6` folder from
the source code of this chapter.

We will not implement the web service method for a DELETE HTTP request as it is
not required in the main example, but it is an easy task to do if needed.

# Merging PUT and POST request DTOs

The previous examples for POST and PUT web services used request DTOs that
might seem redundant on closer inspection. They expose the bicycle object as a
nested property to showcase the compound validation features and allow reuse of
the payload. The request DTOs served their purpose and can be merged into a single
object, and that object is the `Bicycle` class itself. We can change the class declaration
to the following:

```
[Route("/bicycles", "POST")]
[Route("/bicycles/{Id}", "PUT")]
public class Bicycle : IReturn<Bicycle>
```

We can now safely remove the request DTOs and request DTO validators and leave just the `BicycleValidator` class in place. Because `Bicycle` is a web service method parameter, we don't need to manually register the validator as a dependency in `AppHost.Configure` anymore.

You can explore the updated example in the project found in the `Example6Reduced` folder from the source code of this chapter.

# Calling RESTful web services in AngularJS using the ngResource module

All web service methods are now available for the **Bicycles** application view. We can start integrating the AngularJS application with the web services endpoints. This process will initially reduce the functionality from the previous chapter, but the material covered in this book should allow you to rebuild it using web services this time around.

## Using the $resource service

The AngularJS module `ngResource` is created to provide functionality for interaction with RESTful web services using its `$resource` service. Installing this module is similar to installing `ngRoute` in the previous chapter, as shown in the following command:

```
Install-Package AngularJS.Resource -Version 1.2.15
```

After this, we have to update the `index.html` file and the application module definition to add references to the `ngResource` module. We can now modify the `bicyclesService.js` file and make the required changes for web services integration. We will use the `$resource` service to create a class definition that represents a RESTful web service resource. The resource class will be used to receive and send data from a RESTful web service in two ways: through class methods (static methods) and through class instance methods. All methods will be translated into HTTP requests that will use a specific URL and HTTP verb. The resource class definition is shown in the following code:

```
var BicycleResource = $resource('bicycles/:bicycleId', null,
{
  'update': { method: 'PUT' }
});
```

Note the Pascal-cased variable name, which is specific for a class definition in JavaScript.

The first `$resource` parameter is the URL of the resource that has an optional `:bicycleId` URL parameter. When a web service request is performed, its URL will resolve to `/bicycles/2` or `/bicycles` depending on whether the `:bicycleId` URL parameter is specified or not.

The second parameter is an optional object representing the resource URL default parameters. If we would have passed an object like `{ bicycleId: 3, search: 'modern' }` instead of a `null` object, the resulting base URL used for any web service request would have been `/bicycles/3?search=modern`. Any default parameter that is not a URL parameter will be added to the URL as a query string name and value pair.

The third parameter configures the list of actions that the resource class supports. These actions map to the resource methods we mentioned above, and there are five such built-in actions: `get`, `query`, `save`, `remove`, and `delete`. The first two are available as class methods and the last three are available as class instance methods that need to be prefixed with the `$` character when called. These built-in actions don't need to be specified explicitly unless they need to be customized. The extra action that is specified in the third parameter allows us to make PUT requests as they are not available by default in the resource class.

# Resource class methods

The `BicycleResource` class methods return a resource class instance (`get`) or a collection of resource class instances (`query`). The returned objects are initially empty and are populated with data returned by the web service asynchronously. The following code shows the class methods in action in the updated `bicyclesService` code snippet that is now using the `BicycleResource` class to return an array of bicycles or an individual bicycle:

```
getBicycles: function () {
  return BicycleResource.query();
},
getBicycle: function (bicycleId) {
  return BicycleResource.get({ bicycleId: bicycleId });
},
```

You can find the full example for this section in the project found in the `Example7` folder from the source code of this chapter.

The objects returned by the resource class methods are also instances of the `BicycleResource` class. Because of this, they have an additional property named `$promise` to allow for additional code to be executed when the web service request is finished. The `$promise` property is an object that provides access to the result or the error of an asynchronous operation. This object is called a **promise** and it has three methods that can be used to execute code when the asynchronous operation has returned a result (was resolved) or has encountered an error (was rejected): `then`, `catch`, and `finally`. These methods have at least one function parameter that will be executed when the asynchronous operation has finished with a result or an error. The `then` method also returns a promise object, allowing for the creation of chains of promises that can execute code sequentially after each promise in the chain has been resolved or rejected.

 A promise instance can also be stored for later retrieval or be reused throughout the application. More details about the AngularJS promise API can be found at http://code.angularjs.org/1.2.15/ docs/api/ng/service/$q.

AngularJS will ensure that all resource instances or arrays of instances that are also scope properties will update the view when their associated promise object is resolved. Going back to our main example application, the `bicyclesController.js` file doesn't need to be changed because the view will be updated automatically when the result returned by the `bicyclesService.getBicycles()` call is resolved.

For the `bicycleController.js` file, we have to make changes to the code executed after we load an existing bicycle, as shown in the following code:

```
$scope.formTitle = "Update bicycle";
originalBicycle =
bicyclesService.getBicycle($routeParams.bicycleId);
originalBicycle.$promise.then(function () {
  $scope.bicycle = angular.copy(originalBicycle);
});
```

Note how we pass a function to the `$promise.then` method that wraps the previous code that needs to be executed after the bicycle object is available.

# Resource instance methods

The three built-in instance methods of the resource class (save, delete, and remove) will return a promise object directly when executed. The instance data is automatically populated when the promise is resolved. The code from this chapter only uses the save method that will use the HTTP verb POST for the web service request.

When we create a new bicycle entry in bicyclesService, we need to return an instance of the BicycleResource class so we can call the save method to send the new bicycle object back to the server. The code for this operation is as follows:

```
createBicycle: function () {
  return new BicycleResource({
      type: bicycleTypes[0].id,
      typeName: bicycleTypes[0].name,
      quantity: 1,
      rentPrice: 10
  });
},
```

Subsequently, the code that persists the new bicycle to the server is changed to the following code:

```
addBicycle: function (bicycle) {
  updateBicycleTypeName(bicycle);
  return bicycle.$save();
},
```

Note that the method returns a promise object now, so the BicycleController code calling it needs to be changed to the following code:

```
bicyclesService
 .addBicycle($scope.bicycle)
 .then(function () {
      $location.path('/bicycles');
 });
```

# Custom resource methods

When we update an existing bicycle entry, we need to send a PUT HTTP request to the server. The resource class does not have any built-in method matching this HTTP verb and it needs a new custom resource method to be configured.

The resource class definition has a third parameter, which is a configuration object defining the new `update` custom method. Any custom resource method will be a class method rather than an instance method.

The `bicyclesService` service code that sends an existing bicycle entry back to the server for persistence is changed to the following code:

```
updateBicycle: function (bicycle) {
  updateBicycleTypeName(bicycle);
  return BicycleResource.update({ bicycleId: bicycle.id }, bicycle);
}
```

Note that the custom resource method is called in a similar manner with the built-in `get` method. The difference is in the bicycle object to be updated, which is specified as a second parameter. The `BicycleController` code calling this method is changed to the following:

```
angular.copy($scope.bicycle, originalBicycle);
originalBicycle = bicyclesService.updateBicycle(originalBicycle);
originalBicycle.$promise.then(function () {
  $location.path('/bicycles');
});
```

We have now updated the **Bicycles** view functionality to use the ServiceStack-powered web services. If you run the last example, you will see that any changed data is persisted when the browser page is refreshed and not cleared, like in the last example from the previous chapter.

# Summary

This chapter introduced RESTful web service frameworks and showed you how to implement web services for an AngularJS application. It also showed how to use AngularJS components to make HTTP requests for these web services, and how to execute application logic when the HTTP requests are completed, with the use of the promise API.

The next chapter will discuss the integration with ASP.NET MVC and introduce data persistence to the sample application.

# 4

# Creating an AngularJS, ASP.NET MVC, ServiceStack Application

In the previous chapter, we learned how to build the first web services to support an AngularJS application. In this chapter, we will learn about the following topics:

- How to integrate an AngularJS application with ASP.NET MVC and ServiceStack

- ASP.NET MVC features that are relevant to AngularJS

- When you need to combine ASP.NET MVC and AngularJS

- How to set up routing with ASP.NET MVC

- How to secure AngularJS applications

- AngularJS and backend integration

- Adding database persistence with ServiceStack

This chapter assumes that you are familiar with the fundamentals of ASP.NET MVC. The last topic of this chapter that deals with database persistence also assumes you have a knowledge of relational databases, .NET data access fundamentals, and **Object-relational Mapping (ORM)** concepts.

Examples from this chapter can also be found as source control repositories hosted online. Examples 1 to 11 can be found at `https://github.com/popalexandruvasile/rentthatbike/` as branches of the main repository (`chapter4-example1` to `chapter4-example11`).

# Using ASP.NET MVC as the application backbone

When ASP.NET MVC was initially launched in 2009, it was the first .NET framework of any kind to have consistent support for unit testing. It came with official documentation on how to implement tests for controllers. It also embraced established design patterns such as MVC and inspired a new wave of web applications that were built in the vein of HTTP, HTML, and CSS, rather than abstracting them away. All this makes ASP.NET MVC a good base to build modern, server-side web applications and brings it conceptually close to JavaScript MVC frameworks such as AngularJS.

# Why you should use ASP.NET MVC

AngularJS applications work best with modern browsers that support HTML5. Although AngularJS 1.2 supports Internet Explorer 8, you need to perform additional work to support older Internet Explorer versions. Moreover, this is where ASP.NET MVC can prove very useful by supporting the following alternative approaches when your application is loaded in a browser that does not fully support AngularJS:

- You can detect whether the browser is unsupported and redirect to an alternative landing page
- You can provide server-side-rendered views that will provide some (if not all) of the AngularJS application functionality

ASP.NET MVC can also deliver the following specific functionality:

- If your application needs to be secured, server-side-rendered views will authenticate the user and ensure that the AngularJS application only loads for authenticated users
- Inject data from the server side into the rendered view and ensure that the AngularJS application loads the data when it starts without requiring an extra web service call
- If the starting page of your application is a server-side view, you can use the Microsoft ASP.NET Web Optimization Framework to bundle and minify your assets

 You can also use an alternative tool called Bundler, developed by the author of ServiceStack, which also integrates with ASP. NET MVC and Visual Studio. More details can be found at https://github.com/ServiceStack/Bundler/.

- You can build hybrid applications, where parts are built using both ASP.NET MVC and AngularJS

Of course, nothing is stopping you from using ASP.NET Web Forms, WCF, or even ASP.NET Web Services in combination with AngularJS, if this is a scenario you need to support.

# Adding ASP.NET MVC to the main sample application

We will now start modifying the main sample application, *Rent That Bike!*, built in the previous chapter and add ASP.NET MVC support to it.

 Since we are using ServiceStack v3, which can run on .NET 3.5, the lowest ASP.NET MVC version it supports is 2.0.

We will use the last ASP.NET MVC version available when the book was written, which is 5.1.2, and we will run the following NuGet Package Manager Console command to add it to our project:

```
Install-Package Microsoft.AspNet.Mvc -Version 5.1.2
```

The next step is to add the minimum set of files required to bootstrap an ASP.NET MVC application. The previous `index.html` file becomes a server-side, rendered view for the `Index` action of the `HomeController` class. Most of the HTML found on the `index.html` page is moved to the `_Layout.cshtml` file. All of the script references will have to slightly be changed to the format expected by ASP.NET MVC. The server-side web application has a single controller that will be tasked with generating the initial view that contains the client-side application rendered by AngularJS.

To accomplish a similar setup, you can either look at a default ASP.NET MVC project and extract the differences or start with an ASP.NET MVC project and add the AngularJS files. You can explore all of the changes in the `Example1` folder from the source code for this chapter.

# Integrating ASP.NET MVC with ServiceStack

ServiceStack was initially set up to serve any requests for resources from the root of the web application, that is, `localhost:61803/bicycles`. Since this clashes with the ASP.NET MVC routing, we need to move the ServiceStack web services to an `api` virtual path so it can serve requests such as `localhost:61803/api/bicycles`. We need to change the following files in our project:

1. Move the HTTP handler ServiceStack registration to the `api` virtual folder. The following code is the new `web.config` node that replaces the previous registration:

```
<location path="api">
    <system.webServer>
      <handlers>
        <add path="*" name="ServiceStack.Factory"
type="ServiceStack.WebHost.Endpoints.ServiceStackHttpHandle
rFactory, ServiceStack" verb="*"
preCondition="integratedMode"
resourceType="Unspecified" allowPathInfo="true" />
      </handlers>
    </system.webServer>
</location>
```

2. Change the endpoint configuration for ServiceStack in the `AppHost.Configure` method so it will use the new `api` virtual path as follows:

```
public override void Configure(Container container)
        {
            SetConfig(CreateEndpointHostConfig());

            JsConfig.EmitCamelCaseNames = true;

            Plugins.Add(new ValidationFeature());
            container.RegisterValidators(typeof(AppHost).
Assembly);

            container.RegisterAutoWired<BicycleRepository>();
        }

        protected virtual EndpointHostConfig
CreateEndpointHostConfig()
        {
            return new EndpointHostConfig
            {
```

```
              DebugMode = true,
              DefaultContentType = ContentType.Json,
              ServiceStackHandlerFactoryPath = "api"
          };
      }
```

3.  Adjust the ASP.NET MVC routing so it ignores any requests to the `api` virtual folder. The `RouteConfig.cs` file needs the following line to be added:

```
routes.IgnoreRoute("api/{*pathInfo}");
```

4.  And finally, the `bicyclesService.js` file needs to point to the new web service path as shown in the following code:

```
var BicycleResource = $resource('api/bicycles/:bicycleId',
null,
      {
          'update': { method: 'PUT' }
      });
```

At this point, we hit a new milestone by integrating ASP.NET MVC with AngularJS and ServiceStack. It was a manual process for me, but you can alternatively start with an ASP.NET MVC project first and add AngularJS and the NuGet package called ServiceStack.Mvc to set up integration with ServiceStack.

You can explore all of these changes in the same `Example1` folder from the source code for this chapter.

# Routing considerations for ASP.NET MVC and AngularJS

In the previous example, we had to make changes to the ASP.NET MVC routing so it ignores the requests handled by the ServiceStack framework. Since the AngularJS application currently uses hashbang URLs, we don't need to make any other changes to the ASP.NET MVC routing.

Changing an AngularJS application to use the HTML5 History API instead of hashbang URLs requires a lot more work as it will conflict directly with the ASP. NET MVC routing. You need to set up IIS URL rewriting and use the URL Rewrite module for IIS 7 and higher, which is available at `www.iis.net/downloads/ microsoft/url-rewrite`. AngularJS application routes have to be mapped using this module to the ASP.NET MVC view that hosts the client-side application. We also need to ensure that web service request paths are excluded from URL rewriting.

You can explore some changes required for the HTML5 navigation mode in the project found in the Example2 folder from the source code for this chapter. However, since setting up the HTML5 navigation mode on both the server side and client side is complex, we will use hashbang-URL-based navigation throughout the book.

> The HTML5 History API is not supported in Internet Explorer 8 and 9.

# Using ASP.NET bundling and minification features for AngularJS files

So far, we have referenced and included JavaScript and CSS files directly in the _Layout.cshtml file. This makes it difficult to reuse script references between different views, and the assets are not concatenated and minified when deployed to a production environment. Microsoft provides a NuGet package called Microsoft. AspNet.Web.Optimization that contains this essential functionality. When you create a new ASP.NET MVC project, it gets installed and configured with default options. For our main sample application, we will configure this library manually by integrating existing scripts and style sheets and preparing the ground for further additions in later chapters.

First, we need to add a new BundleConfig.cs file, which will define collections of scripts and style sheets under a virtual path, such as ~/bundles/app, that does not match a physical file. This file will contain the following code:

```
bundles.Add(new ScriptBundle("~/bundles/app").Include(
    "~/scripts/app/app.js",
    "~/scripts/app/services/*.js",
    "~/scripts/app/controllers/*.js"));
```

You can explore these changes in the project found in the Example3 folder from the source code for this chapter. If you take a look at the BundleConfig.cs file, you will see three script bundles and one style sheet bundle defined. Nothing is stopping you from defining only one script bundle instead, to reduce the resource requests further.

We can now reference the bundles in the _Layout.cshtml file and replace the previous scripts with the following code:

```
@Scripts.Render("~/bundles/basejs")
@Scripts.Render("~/bundles/angular")
@Scripts.Render("~/bundles/app")
```

Each time we add a new file to a location like ~/scripts/app/services/ it will automatically be included in its bundle. If we add the following line of code to the BundleConfig.RegisterBundles method, when we run the application, the scripts or style sheets defined in a bundle will be minified (all of the whitespace, line separators, and comments will be removed) and concatenated in a single file:

```
BundleTable.EnableOptimizations = true;
```

If we take a look at the page source, the script section now looks like the following code:

```
<script src="/bundles/basejs?v=bWXds_q0E1qezGAjF9o48iD8-
hlMNv7nlAONwLLM0Wo1"></script>
<script src="/bundles/angular?v=k-
PtTeaKyBiBwT4gVnEq9YTPNruD0u7n13IOEzGTvfw1"></script>
<script
src="/bundles/app?v=OKa5fFQWjXSQCNcBuWm9FJLcPFS8hGM6uq1SIdZNXWc1"></
script>
```

Using this process, the previous separate requests for each script or style sheet file will be reduced to a request to one or more bundles that are much reduced in content due to concatenation and minification.

For convenience, there is a new EnableOptimizations value in web.config that will enable or disable the concatenation and minification of the asset bundles.

# Securing the AngularJS application

We previously discussed that we need to ensure that all browser requests are secured and validated on the server for specific scenarios. Any browser request can be manipulated and changed even unintentionally, so we cannot rely on client-side validation alone.

When discussing securing an AngularJS application, there are a couple of alternatives available, of which I'll mention the following:

- You can use client-side authentication and employ a web service call to authenticate the current user. You can create a time-limited authentication token that will be passed with each data request. This approach involves additional code in the AngularJS application to handle authentication.

- You can rely on server-side authentication and use an ASP.NET MVC view that will handle any unauthenticated request. This view will redirect to the view that hosts the AngularJS application only when the authentication is successful. The AngularJS application will implicitly use an authentication cookie that is set on the server side, and it does not need any additional code to handle authentication.

I prefer server-side authentication as it can be reused with other server-side views and reduces the code required to implement it on both the client side and server side. We can implement server-side authentication in at least two ways, as follows:

- We can use the ASP.NET Identity system or the older ASP.NET Membership system for scenarios where we need to integrate with an existing application

- We can use built-in ServiceStack authentication features, which have a wide range of options with support for many authentication providers. This approach has the benefit that we can add a set of web service methods that can be used for authentication outside of the ASP.NET MVC context.

The last approach ensures the best integration between ASP.NET MVC and ServiceStack, and it allows us to introduce a ServiceStack NuGet package that provides new productivity benefits for our sample application.

# Using the ServiceStack.Mvc library

ServiceStack has a library that allows deeper integration with ASP.NET MVC through the ServiceStack.Mvc NuGet package. This library provides access to the ServiceStack dependency injection system for ASP.NET MVC applications. It also introduces a new base controller class called `ServiceStackController`; this can be used by ASP.NET MVC controllers to gain access to the ServiceStack caching, session, and authentication infrastructures. To install this package, you need to run the following command in the NuGet Package Manager Console:

```
Install-Package ServiceStack.Mvc -Version 3.9.71
```

The following line needs to be added to the `AppHost.Configure` method, and it will register a ServiceStack controller factory class for ASP.NET MVC:

```
ControllerBuilder.Current.SetControllerFactory(new
FunqControllerFactory(container));
```

The `ControllerBuilder.Current.SetControllerFactory` method is an ASP.NET MVC extension point that allows the replacement of its `DefaultControllerFactory` class with a custom one. This class is tasked with matching requests with controllers, among other responsibilities. The `FunqControllerFactory` class provided in the new NuGet package inherits the `DefaultControllerFactory` class and ensures that all controllers that have dependencies managed by the ServiceStack dependency injection system will be resolved at application runtime.

To exemplify this, the `BicycleRepository` class is now referenced in the `HomeController` class, as shown in the following code:

```
public class HomeController : Controller
{
  public BicycleRepository BicycleRepository { get; set; }

  //
  // GET: /Home/
  public ActionResult Index()
  {
      ViewBag.BicyclesCount = BicycleRepository.GetAll().Count();
      return View();
  }
}
```

The application menu now displays the current number of bicycles as initialized in the `BicycleRepository` class. If we add a new bicycle and refresh the browser page, the menu bicycle count is updated. This highlights the fact that the ASP.NET MVC application uses the same `BicycleRepository` instance as ServiceStack web services.

You can explore this example in the project found in the `Example4` folder from the source code for this chapter.

Using the ServiceStack.Mvc library, we have reached a new milestone by bridging ASP.NET MVC controllers with ServiceStack services. In the next section, we will effectively transition to a single server-side application with unified caching, session, and authentication infrastructures.

# The building blocks of the ServiceStack security infrastructure

ServiceStack has built-in, optional authentication and authorization provided by its AuthFeature plugin, which builds on two other important components as follows:

- **Caching**: Every service or controller powered by ServiceStack has optional access to an ICacheClient interface instance that provides cache-related methods. The interface needs to be registered as an instance of one of the many caching providers available: an in-memory cache, a relational database cache, a cache based on a key value data store using Redis, a memcached-based cache, a Microsoft Azure cache, and even a cache based on Amazon DynamoDB.

- **Sessions**: These are enabled by the SessionFeature ServiceStack plugin and rely on the caching component when the AuthFeature plugin is not enabled. Every service or controller powered by ServiceStack has an ISession property that provides read and write access to the session data. Each ServiceStack request automatically has two cookies set: an ss-id cookie, which is a regular session cookie, and an ss-pid cookie, which is a permanent cookie with an expiry date set far in the future. You can also gain access to a typed session as part of the AuthFeature plugin that will be explored next.

# Introducing the AuthFeature plugin

The AuthFeature plugin builds on the plugins we mentioned earlier as it requires an ICacheClient dependency to be registered, and it automatically enables the SessionFeature plugin. When registering the AuthFeature plugin, at least two interface instances need to be provided as part of the plugin definition, as follows:

- An IAuthSession instance that represents the user data associated with the request session, also known as a typed session, needs to be provided. The IAuthSession interface has properties such as Id, UserName, DisplayName, and Email and methods such as OnAuthenticated and OnLogout. It is a minimal interface that will be used by all ServiceStack authentication providers.

- One or more instances of the IAuthProvider interface, which represents a ServiceStack authentication provider, need to be supplied. The interface contains a minimum set of properties, such as AuthRealm, that will be used by ServiceStack to set up a web service endpoint; this will perform authentication checks. The interface also has methods such as Authenticate, which will perform the actual authentication.

ServiceStack comes with a default implementation for the `IAuthSession` interface in the `AuthUserSession` class, which contains some additional properties that are relevant for the different authentication providers that are available. The following providers are the default authentication providers that implement the `IAuthProvider` interface:

- `CredentialsAuthProvider` allows username- and password-based authentication and is the one we will explore in this book

- `BasicAuthProvider` and `DigestAuthProvider` enable HTTP basic and digest access authentication

- OAuth-based providers such as `TwitterAuthProvider` and `FacebookAuthProvider`

- OpenId- and OAuth2-based providers are available as part of the NuGet packages ServiceStack.Authentication.OpenId and ServiceStack.Authentication.OAuth2

We will use `CredentialsAuthProvider` as the preferred authentication provider in this application because it is the closest match to the forms-based authentication feature from ASP.NET.

Authentication in ServiceStack also has a data persistence configuration element that needs to be initialized. Properties for the `IAuthSession` interface and the class that implements it (`AuthUserSession`, as used in the main sample in this book) need to be persisted through an instance that implements the `IUserAuthRepository` interface. This interface contains method definitions that will be used by the `AuthFeature` plugin to store or retrieve user data and authenticate a user against the data store. There are a couple of default implementations for this interface, such as `InMemoryAuthRepository`, which persists data in memory and will be used in the next example; `OrmLiteAuthRepository`, which persists data using the ServiceStack micro ORM library OrmLite; and `RedisAuthRepository`, which uses the Redis database for storage.

Additional support for data persistence with MongoDB and RavenDB databases and through the NHibernate ORM is provided through the NuGet packages, ServiceStack.Authentication. MongoDB, ServiceStack.Authentication.RavenDB, and ServiceStack. Authentication.NHibernate.

# Implementing authentication for web services

We will now change the main sample application to enable and use the `AuthFeature` plugin by adding the following lines to the `AppHost.Configure` method:

```
Plugins.Add(new AuthFeature(
    () => new AuthUserSession(),
  new IAuthProvider[] {
        new CredentialsAuthProvider()
    }));
var userAuthRepository = new InMemoryAuthRepository();
userAuthRepository.CreateUserAuth(new UserAuth { Email =
"admin@rentthatbike.com", DisplayName= "Admin User"}, "admin");
container.Register<IUserAuthRepository>(userAuthRepository);
```

Note how we added the initial user data using `CreateUserAuth`, one of the `IUserAuthRepository` interface methods. The `Email` property was used instead of the `UserName` property to establish the user login name as they are both supported—if `UserName` is not set, then the `Email` property will be used instead when performing the authentication check.

The addition of `CredentialsAuthProvider` makes a new web service endpoint available, which can be tested using Postman at the address `localhost:61803/api/auth/credentials`. If we send the next JSON payload using a POST request, the authentication check will be performed as shown in the following code:

```
{
  "userName": "admin@rentthatbike.com",
  "password": "admin"
}
```

Even if we specified the `Email` property when the initial user data was persisted, we still have to use a `UserName` property for the authentication service endpoint. If we enable the Interceptor plugin in Postman, we will see the cookies that were set for the request, namely, `ss-id` and `ss-pid`, as expected.

The next step is to enforce authentication in the `BicycleService` class. If we add the `AuthenticateAttribute` declaration for the class definition as shown in the following code, the web service will be accessible only for requests that are part of an authenticated session:

```
[Authenticate]
public class BicyclesService : IService
```

You can explore the example in the project found in the `Example5` folder from the source code for this chapter.

# Implementing authentication for ASP.NET MVC controllers

If the main sample had been just a single-page application, as explored in the previous chapter, we would have stopped here and moved to the next topic. Given the ASP. NET MVC integration, we now have to extend the authentication to the controllers and ensure that they are secured as well. We need to secure the HomeController class and redirect any unauthenticated requests to a new login page.

Securing the controller is just a matter of inheriting from ServiceStackController and adding the AuthenticateAttribute declaration to the controller class. When the AuthFeature plugin is enabled, it registers a default, redirect route set to ~/login. We will match this route by creating a LoginController class with an Index method. When an unauthenticated request is processed by HomeController, it will be redirected to the default login page with the previous route passed as a query string value, localhost:61803/login?redirect=%2f.

The login page is a simple ASP.NET MVC view that does not have any AngularJS references and only shows minimal content using a Bootstrap-powered HTML layout, as showcased at http://getbootstrap.com/examples/signin/. A new layout file, _LayoutMinimal.cshtml, was created that contains references to the style sheet bundle and the basejs bundle. The Index.cshtml file contains the login form associated with a LoginData model and ensures that data is posted to the LogIn controller method when the form is submitted. The following code depicts this:

```
@model RentThatBike.Web.Models.LoginData
@{
    Layout = "~/Views/Shared/_LayoutMinimal.cshtml";
    ViewBag.Title = "Log in to Rent That Bike!";
}
<div class="container">
    @using (Html.BeginForm("LogIn", "Login", FormMethod.Post, new
{ @class = "form-signin", role = "form" }))
    {
        <h2 class="form-signin-heading">Please log in</h2>
        @Html.HiddenFor(m => m.Redirect)
        @Html.ValidationSummary()
        @Html.TextBoxFor(m => m.EmailAddress, new { type =
"email", @class = "form-control", placeholder = "Email Address",
required = "", autofocus = "" })
        @Html.TextBoxFor(m => m.Password, new { type = "password",
@class = "form-control", placeholder = "Password", required =
"required" })
```

```
        <label class="checkbox">
            @Html.CheckBoxFor(m => m.RememberMe) Remember me
        </label>
        <button class="btn btn-lg btn-primary btn-block"
type="submit">Log in</button>
    }
</div>
```

The `LoginController.Index` method passes the query string `redirect` parameter value to the hidden input from the preceding markup, as shown in the following code:

```
[HttpGet]
public ActionResult Index(string redirect)
{
    return View(new LoginData{Redirect = redirect});
}
```

This way, when the form is posted, we are able to redirect to the correct route if the authentication is successful, as shown in the `LoginController.LogIn` method in the following code:

```
public AuthService AuthService { get; set; }
[HttpPost]
public ActionResult LogIn(LoginData loginData)
{
    if (!ModelState.IsValid)
    {
        return View("Index", loginData);
    }
    AuthService.RequestContext =
System.Web.HttpContext.Current.ToRequestContext();
    try
    {
        AuthResponse authResponse = AuthService.Authenticate(new
Auth
        {
            UserName = loginData.EmailAddress,
            Password = loginData.Password,
            RememberMe = loginData.RememberMe,
            Continue = loginData.Redirect
        });

        return Redirect(loginData.Redirect);
    }
```

```
catch (HttpError ex)
{
    if (ex.Status == 401)
    {
        ModelState.AddModelError("", ex.ErrorCode);
        return View("Index", loginData);
    }
    throw;
}
}
```

Note how we registered `AuthService` as a controller dependency by simply declaring it as a public property. We then used it to perform the authentication that was relayed to the `CredentialsAuthProvider` instance. If the authentication is successful, we get redirected to the / route. After this point, if we load the **Bicycles** application view and check the cookies associated with the / request and the `api/ bicycles` request, we will notice they have the same `ss-id` value. All of the requests will share the same session from now on.

If we look at the project found in the `Example5` folder from the source code for this chapter, we notice that the `HomeController` class inherits from the `ServiceStackCo ntroller<AuthUserSession>` class. Using this base class gives us access to the typed session instance represented by `AuthUserSession` through the controller base class property, `UserSession`. We can now display the user details from the typed session in the application menu by storing them in the `HomeController.ViewBag` property and adding them to the menu in `_Layout.chtml`, as shown in the following code:

```
<ul class="nav navbar-nav navbar-right">
  <li><a href="#">@ViewBag.AuthUserSession.DisplayName</a></li>
</ul>
```

The following screenshot shows how the application menu looks now after a user gets authenticated:

ServiceStack supports more security features; they are as follows:

- Authorization through roles and permissions
- Using a global filter to enforce authentication
- Automatic user registration through the `RegistrationFeature` plugin

 You can find more information about these features for ServiceStack 3.9 at `https://github.com/ServiceStackV3/ServiceStackV3/wiki/Authentication-and-authorization` and for ServiceStack 4.0 at `https://github.com/ServiceStack/ServiceStack/wiki/Authentication-and-authorization`.

# Pushing initial data from the server-side application to the AngularJS application

A single-page application that does not have a server-side framework gets its data exclusively through web service calls. Using a framework such as ASP.NET MVC enables us to push server-side data to the AngularJS application, eliminating the need for an initial web service call. This is especially useful when the data that needs to be pushed is already available, such as the authenticated user details. To showcase this approach, we push the current user details to the AngularJS application, which uses these to render the authenticated user information and replace existing server-side functionality.

We can use a simple but effective technique where the server-side data is set as an AngularJS constant called `serverSideData`, defined in the `_Layout.cshtml` file. First, we need to prepare the source data represented by the `ServerSideData` class, initialized in the `HomeController.Index` method, as shown in the following code:

```
public ActionResult Index()
{
  ViewBag.AuthUserSession = UserSession;

  ViewBag.ServerSideDataAsJson = new ServerSideData
  {
      UserDisplayName = UserSession.DisplayName,
      UserEmail = UserSession.Email
  }.ToJson();

  return View();
}
```

We just copy the relevant user session properties and convert the `ServerSideData` instance to a JSON string using the `ToJson` extension method of the ServiceStack. Text library. This way, we ensure that any JSON-formatted data uses the same serialization options as the web service methods.

The `script` section of the `_Layout.cshtml` file can be modified to include the AngularJS new constant definition as follows:

```
@Scripts.Render("~/bundles/app")
<script type="text/javascript">
  (function() {
      "use strict";
      var myAppModule = angular.module('myApp');
      myAppModule.constant("serverSideData",
@Html.Raw(ViewBag.ServerSideDataAsJson) );
  })();
</script>
@RenderSection("scripts", required: false)
```

We had to use the `Html.Raw` method to avoid the HTML encoding of the inline JSON string. The `serverSideData` AngularJS constant is now available to the client-side application, and we can modify the `applicationController.js` file to add the constant to its scope, as follows:

```
myAppModule.controller('ApplicationController', ['$scope',
'serverSideData',
    function ($scope, serverSideData) {
        $scope.isMainMenuCollapsed = false;
        $scope.serverSideData = serverSideData;
    }
]);
```

As a final step, we go back to the `_Layout.cshtml` file and change the application menu markup to use the new `ApplicationController` scope property to render the user details, as shown in the following code:

```
<div class="collapse navbar-collapse" data-
collapse="isMainMenuCollapsed">
  <ul class="nav navbar-nav">
      <li><a href="#/rentals">Rentals</a></li>
      <li><a href="#/customers">Customers</a></li>
      <li><a href="#/bicycles">Bicycles</a></li>
  </ul>
  <ul class="nav navbar-nav navbar-right">
      <li><a
href="#">{{serverSideData.userDisplayName}}({{serverSideData.userE
mail}})</a></li>
  </ul>
</div>
```

We can easily imagine a scenario where we push more complex data that can be used by AngularJS to initialize the application quicker and minimize the waiting time until the initial application view is fully loaded.

# How to ensure that AngularJS works well with the backend

In the previous chapter, we introduced some of the web service methods that support AngularJS applications with very few code modifications compared to the implementation without web services. We chose to ignore some inherent complications associated with calling web services, but now we will address them in the following sections.

## Handling the waiting time for long operations

Calling a web service method usually has an overhead that is caused by the transport of data to and from the server. When the data operations are also relatively expensive on the server, your application might end up waiting for data for a duration of time that is perceived as significant by the user. In this scenario, you need to ensure that the user gets notified that the application is currently performing an expensive operation and it might take a while. There are a couple of user interface elements that can be used to implement the wait notifications and are available as AngularJS modules, as follows:

- **angular-spinner**: This provides a spinner animation, most suitable for relatively fast operations without a fixed duration, such as web service calls. The JavaScript library, spin.js, implements a configurable animation that can be used in AngularJS applications, thanks to the angular-spinner module found at `https://github.com/urish/angular-spinner`.

- **Angular UI Bootstrap**: This provides a progress bar animation, which is a good fit in scenarios where you know the duration of the operation or the operation can be broken up in steps of predictable size. This is available in the Angular UI Bootstrap AngularJS module that is already added to our main sample application. More information on this element can be found at `http://angular-ui.github.io/bootstrap/`.

- **AngularJS Toaster**: This provides a "toast" notification, which is useful for operations with a long duration or for "fire and forget" operations. A popular JavaScript library that implements the animation is toastr.js, which has a demo available at `http://codeseven.github.io/toastr/demo.html`. There is an AngularJS port called AngularJS Toaster available at `https://github.com/jirikavi/AngularJS-Toaster`.

We will modify the main sample application to add support for a spinner animation whenever a web service method is called. First, we install the spin.js library through the following NuGet Package Manager Console command:

```
Install-Package-package Spin.js -Version 2.0
```

We then need to install the angular-spinner.js module that does not have a NuGet package yet. A great repository for AngularJS modules that are not yet available on NuGet can be found at `http://ngmodules.org/`, and we will use it to download the `angular-spinner.js` file. We can add it to the AngularJS application by changing the application module definition to the following code:

```
var myAppModule = angular.module('myApp', ['ngRoute',
'ngResource', 'ui.bootstrap', 'angularSpinner']);
```

The new module has a `us-spinner` directive that takes JSON-formatted object properties and generates an animation shaped by these properties using the spin. js library behind the scenes. We added an HTML element with this directive and a `spinner-key` identification attribute above the main application grid, as shown in the following code:

```
<span us-spinner="{radius:20, width:8, length: 15}" spinner-
key="mainSpinner"></span>
<div class="container" ng-view>
</div>
```

We can now modify the `bicyclesController.js` file to reference a service from the same module and use it to start and stop the animation represented by the identification attribute value, as follows:

```
myAppModule.controller('BicyclesController', ['$scope',
'bicyclesService', 'usSpinnerService',
        function ($scope, bicyclesService, usSpinnerService) {
            usSpinnerService.spin("mainSpinner");
            $scope.bicycles = bicyclesService.getBicycles();

            $scope.bicycles.$promise.then(function () {
                usSpinnerService.stop("mainSpinner");
            });
        }
]);
```

You can explore this example in the project found in the `Example7` folder from the source code for this chapter. I added spinner animations to the rest of the web service calls and introduced an artificial delay in the web service response to ensure that the animation is visible for 2 seconds.

# Handling exceptions and implementing generic animations

In *Chapter 2, Creating an AngularJS Client-side Application in Visual Studio*, we implemented a service decorator for the built-in $exceptionHandler service to ensure that any client-side exception is visible in the browser. If a server-side exception occurs, it will still be logged in the browser console and be invisible to the users of the application. To change this behavior, we need to use a new design pattern implemented in AngularJS: the **interceptor**.

## Adding a $http interceptor

All of the services implemented so far rely on the $resource factory to deal with all client-server data transport details. This factory is, in fact, just a wrapper around the lower level $http service that will initiate any HTTP request to the server and process any HTTP response from the server. The $http service is based on the promise interface we discussed in the *Resource instance methods* section of *Chapter 3, Creating .NET Web Services for AngularJS*. The promise interface is provided by another built-in service, $q, which is similar to the established Q JavaScript library that implements the promise specification, Promises/A+, defined at http://promises-aplus.github.io/promises-spec/.

 More details about Q can be found at http://documentup.com/kriskowal/q, and further details about the AngularJS $q service can be found at http://code.angularjs.org/1.2.15/docs/api/ng/service/$q.

The promise interface is a key ingredient to implement the service factory that defines the $http service interceptor. This service factory can contain up to four interceptor functions that can execute code for four separate $http service request and response interception points; they are as follows:

- request: This function is used when the request is configured before being sent

- requestError: This function is used when the request configuration has encountered an error

- response: This function is used when a response is received

- responseError: This function is used when a response error has occurred

The $http service supports many such interceptors that are chained together. It is for this reason that an interceptor implementation needs to deal gracefully with the chain of interceptors by employing the $q service when handling a request or response.

To showcase how a server exception needs to be handled, the BicyclesService class will throw a custom exception when the list of bicycles is retrieved. Implementing $http service interceptors is as simple as defining a new service factory first, as shown in the following code:

```
var serviceId = 'httpInterceptor';
angular.module('myApp').factory(serviceId, ['$q',
'usSpinnerService', httpInterceptor]);
function httpInterceptor($q, usSpinnerService) {
  var service = {
      'responseError': function (rejection) {
          var hasErrorMessage = false;
          var errorMessage;
          // check for generic ServiceStack exception
          if (rejection.data && rejection.data.responseStatus &&
rejection.data.responseStatus.message) {
              hasErrorMessage = true;
              errorMessage =
rejection.data.responseStatus.message;
          }

          if (hasErrorMessage) {
              alert("Http response error: " +
errorMessage);
              usSpinnerService.stop("mainSpinner");
          }

          return $q.reject(rejection);
      }
  };
  return service;
}
```

The syntax of the service factory definition is slightly changed as the Visual Studio extension, SideWaffle Template Pack, was used to generate the service file. The extension separates the service factory declaration from the function that contains its implementation, making it more readable when it contains a long list of dependencies.

For the moment, we only defined an interceptor for the `responseError` extension point. The interceptor receives a `rejection` object that contains the data returned by the web service. Since ServiceStack formats any server exception using JSON and returns it to its caller in this format, we can easily check the response data and extract the specific exception details. We can then display the exception message in the browser window and stop the spinner animation from the same extension point, as illustrated in the highlighted code section.

The last call of the interceptor is to ensure that the response error is passed unchanged to the rest of the chain of interceptors using the `$q` service. To add this interceptor to the `$http` service, the following line of code needs to be added in the app.js file in the first module configuration section:

```
$httpProvider.interceptors.push('httpInterceptor');
```

You can explore the example in the project found in the `Example8` folder from the source code for this chapter.

 More details about the low-level `$http` service and interceptors can be found at `http://code.angularjs.org/1.2.15/docs/api/ng/service/$http`.

## Implementing spinner animations for all web service calls

We already saw in the previous example how we can stop spinner animations when a response exception occurs. We can now easily start and stop spinner animations for all present and future web service calls by implementing the remaining `$http` service interceptors as shown in the following code:

```
'request': function (config) {
  usSpinnerService.spin("mainSpinner");
  return config || $q.when(config);
},
'requestError': function (rejection) {
  usSpinnerService.stop("mainSpinner");
  return $q.reject(rejection);
},
'response': function (response) {
  usSpinnerService.stop("mainSpinner");
  return response || $q.when(response);
},
```

We can see how, after the spinner animation was manipulated, we left calls in place that will ensure that the chain of interceptors still works the way it did before we made our change. There is an artificial delay that is added in the web service to ensure that the animations are always visible. All of the controller code that used to manipulate animations has now been removed.

You can explore this example in the project found in the `Example9` folder from the source code for this chapter.

# Adding database persistence

All of the code examples we have explored so far have used in-memory data stores that are recreated each time the application restarts. It is now time to add support for database persistence so we can progress the main application example towards a production-ready status. We also need to prepare for the next chapter; it will cover testing-related topics that need the database persistence functionality to be in place.

The ServiceStack framework comes with built-in functionality for lightweight ORM functionality in the ServiceStack.OrmLite library. There are established ORM libraries and frameworks, such as Entity Framework and NHibernate, that provide mapping between the .NET type system and relational database objects. They usually incur a performance penalty compared to direct .NET data access, require extensive configuration, have a high learning cost upfront, and might not be suitable for smaller projects or projects that use a simpler database structure. These issues caused the apparition of a new wave of micro-ORM libraries, such as Dapper, Massive, and Simple.Data, that are very fast compared to classic ORM frameworks, are intuitive to use, and simple to configure.

As the main theme of this book is rapid prototyping and development, by using a micro-ORM library, we employ a quick and efficient way to implement database persistence for the main sample application. The ServiceStack.OrmLite library is part of the micro-ORM wave and provides its main functionality as a set of extensions on top of the `System.Data.IDbConnection` interface. It uses one-to-one mapping between a table and class and has a series of data annotation attributes that configure primary and foreign keys, indexes, and other database-related objects. We will explore some of its features in the next section and throughout the rest of the book, where relevant.

> You can find out more about ServiceStack.Ormlite Version 3.9 at `https://github.com/ServiceStack/ServiceStack.OrmLite/tree/v3` and about Version 4 at `https://github.com/ServiceStack/ServiceStack.OrmLite`.

# Adding database persistence to the AuthFeature plugin

The ServiceStack.Ormlite library supports multiple database engines through additional NuGet packages, such as ServiceStack.OrmLite.SqlServer, ServiceStack. OrmLite.Oracle, and ServiceStack.OrmLite.Sqlite32, to name a few. The free and open source SQLite database is of special interest as it is a popular choice as an embedded database engine that doesn't require a separate process or service to be configured. As it implements most of the SQL-92 standard for SQL, it can easily be replaced with another relational database engine, such as Microsoft SQL Server. It also supports an in-memory execution mode, where data is not persisted to a file; this makes it a great choice to implement fast tests, which will be useful in the next chapter.

SQLite comes in two flavors: a 32-bit version and a 64-bit version. To provide support for more Windows operating system platforms and reduce configuration steps, we will change the build configuration of the main application project to target the x86 platform, and we will import the required NuGet package using the following command:

```
Install-Package ServiceStack.OrmLite.Sqlite32 -Version 3.9.71
```

 ServiceStack can also run on Linux and Mac OS X with the Mono C# runtime. There is an OrmLite NuGet package called ServiceStack. OrmLite.Sqlite.Mono that enables SQLite support on these platforms.

With this package installed, we can now add database persistence support to the AuthFeature plugin that we configured in this chapter. First, we need to register the IDbConnectionFactory interface that contains the OpenDbConnection method, which is the main entry point to access the OrmLite functionality. The following code ensures that the interface is resolved to the appropriate SQLite provider in the AppHost.Configure method:

```
container.Register<IDbConnectionFactory>(
  new OrmLiteConnectionFactory(
  ConfigurationManager.ConnectionStrings["SqlLiteConnection"].Connec
tionString.MapAbsolutePath(),
    SqliteDialect.Provider));
```

We use a special connection string in the `web.config` file that points to a named database file, and the built-in ServiceStack `MapAbsolutePath` extension method resolves it relative to the `bin` folder of the web application, as shown in the following code:

```
<connectionStrings>
    <add name="SqlLiteConnection" connectionString
="~/App_Data/rentthatbike.sqlite"/>
  </connectionStrings>
```

In this way, we can avoid any special security configuration for the application folders and host the application on a cloud provider such as Microsoft Azure without any required changes. Anytime that the `bin` folder is cleared (like in an automated deployment scenario), the database file is recreated. This approach is suitable for read-only databases or self-hosted ServiceStack applications, and we will change it to a more robust solution in the next section.

We can change the existing `InMemoryAuthRepository` class to an `OrmLiteAuthRepository` class, which needs the `IDbConnectionFactory` dependency to already be registered, as shown in the following code:

```
container.Register<IUserAuthRepository>(c =>
  new OrmLiteAuthRepository(c.Resolve<IDbConnectionFactory>()));

var userAuthRepository =
(OrmLiteAuthRepository)container.Resolve<IUserAuthRepository>();
userAuthRepository.CreateMissingTables();
if
(userAuthRepository.GetUserAuthByUserName("admin@rentthatbike.com"
) == null)
{
  userAuthRepository.CreateUserAuth(
      new UserAuth {Email = "admin@rentthatbike.com", DisplayName
= "Admin User"}, "admin");
}
```

As the data is now persisted, we need to ensure that the data structure is created through the `CreateMissingTables` method, and we need to verify that the initial user does not exist before trying to create it by calling the `GetUserAuthByUserName` method.

SQLite has a Mozilla Firefox browser plugin called SQLite Manager, available at `http://addons.mozilla.org/en-US/firefox/addon/sqlite-manager`. After we run the application, we can use this plugin to open the `rentthatbike.sqlite` file and inspect the `UserAuth` table, which was created automatically for us and now contains the initial user data as its single row.

You can explore the example in the project found in the `Example10` folder from the source code for this chapter.

# Adding database persistence for web services

Since our sample application is hosted by **Internet Information Services Server Express (IIS Express)**, keeping the database file in the `bin` folder would cause an application restart each time it is updated. As web service methods are expected to change the database file frequently, we need to move its location to the `App_Data` folder in the root folder of the web application. We use another ServiceStack extension method to accomplish this, and our `IDbConnectionFactory` registration now looks like the following code:

```
container.Register<IDbConnectionFactory>(
  new OrmLiteConnectionFactory(
  ConfigurationManager.ConnectionStrings["SqlLiteConnection"].Connec
tionString.MapHostAbsolutePath(),
    SqliteDialect.Provider));
```

The next step is to change the `BicyclesRepository` class and add the `IDbConnectionFactory` interface as a dependency so we can start using ServiceStack.OrmLite features. The `IDbConnectionFactory` interface is used to obtain an `IDbConnection` instance, which is the starting point to implement the database persistence functionality. Without the data access methods, the `BicyclesRepository` class looks like the following code:

```
public class BicycleRepository : IDisposable
{
  public IDbConnectionFactory DbConnectionFactory { get; set; }
  private IDbConnection _db;
  private IDbConnection Db
  {
      get
      {
          return _db ?? (_db = DbConnectionFactory.Open());
      }
  }
  public void Dispose()
  {
```

```
        if (_db != null)
            _db.Dispose();
    }
}
```

The class follows a ServiceStack-recommended approach to ensure that
the IDbConnection instance remains open throughout the lifetime of the
BicyclesRepository instance and gets disposed and implicitly closed
when its parent it disposed. Due to this approach, we cannot register the
BicyclesRepository type with a singleton lifetime scope anymore as the database
connection could remain open indefinitely and we will also start hitting concurrency
issues. We need to change its lifetime scope to Request in AppHost.Configure, as
shown in the following code:

```
container.RegisterAutoWired<BicycleRepository>().ReusedWithin(Reuse
Scope.Request);
```

This means that a new BicyclesRepository instance will be created for each
separate request rather than a single instance being reused within the entire
application lifetime.

You can explore the example for this section and the remaining sections in the
project found in the Example11 folder from the source code for this chapter.

# Persisting the Bicycle class

The next step is to configure the Bicycle class and prepare it for database
persistence. We just need to decorate its properties with ServiceStack.OrmLite
attributes. I will post the entire class definition, as follows, to illustrate how few
changes are required for database persistence support:

```
[Route("/bicycles", "POST")]
[Route("/bicycles/{Id}", "PUT")]
public class Bicycle : IReturn<Bicycle>
{
    [AutoIncrement]
    public int Id { get; set; }

    [Index(Unique = true)]
    public string Name { get; set; }

    public BicycleTypes Type { get; set; }
    public string TypeName
    {
```

```
            get
            {
                return Type.ToString().Replace("Bike", " Bike");
            }
        }
    public int Quantity { get; set; }
    public double RentPrice { get; set; }
}
```

The first highlighted attribute ensures that the property is created as an auto-incrementing primary key table field. The second highlighted attribute creates a unique index for the table field that is mapped to the Name property.

The initial functionality of BicyclesRepository created seed data, and we need to replicate this, with the difference that the code needs to run only if there is no seed data available. ServiceStack.OrmLite provides a CreateTableIfNotExists<T> method, which will create a table for a specific class if that table does not exist. It also has methods such as SqlScalar<T> that support direct SQL queries that return a single value. We can replace the seed data generation code with the AppHost. InitializeDatabase method, which will be called in AppHost.Configure, as shown in the following code:

```
private void InitializeDatabase(Container container)
{
  using (IDbConnection db =
container.Resolve<IDbConnectionFactory>().OpenDbConnection())
    {
        db.CreateTableIfNotExists<Bicycle>();
        if (db.SqlScalar<int>("SELECT COUNT(*) FROM Bicycle") ==
0)
        {
            db.InsertAll(
                new[] {
                new Bicycle { Name = "Very fast bike", Type
= BicycleTypes.RoadBike, Quantity = 5, RentPrice = 15 },
                new Bicycle { Name = "Very springy bike",
Type = BicycleTypes.MountainBike, Quantity = 20, RentPrice = 17 },
                new Bicycle { Name = "Very classy bike",
Type = BicycleTypes.UrbanBike, Quantity = 20, RentPrice = 14 },
                new Bicycle { Name = "Very colorful bike", Type =
BicycleTypes.ChildrenBike, Quantity = 20, RentPrice = 9 }
            });
        }
    }
}
```

The `CreateTableIfNotExists<Bicycle>` creates a table called `Bicycle` with fields that match the class definition and the database object specified in the class property attributes. The next line uses a direct SQL query to check for existing seed data (or any data). The convenient `InsertAll` method ensures that a range of `Bicycle` instances are persisted to the database all at once. Note that we don't need to specify the `Id` property anymore, as it will be generated by the database automatically.

# Changing BicycleRepository to use the OrmLite API

With the database persistence in place, we can now return to `BicycleRepository` and convert its `GetAll`, `Get`, and `Single` methods to use the `Db` instance and its methods. We end up with very concise class methods, as shown in the following code snippet:

```
public List<Bicycle> GetAll()
{
   return Db.Select<Bicycle>();
}
public List<Bicycle> Get(Expression<Func<Bicycle, bool>>
condition)
{
   return Db.Select<Bicycle>(condition);
}
public Bicycle Single(Expression<Func<Bicycle, bool>> condition)
{
   return Db.Select<Bicycle>(condition).Single();
}
```

All changed methods rely on the versatile ServiceStack.OrmLite `Select<T>` method, which accepts an `Expression<Func<T, bool>>` parameter. There are other `Select<T>` methods available, and one of them takes an optionally formatted string similar to the `String.Format` method that allows more complex database queries, as shown in the following code:

```
public static List<T> Select<T>(this IDbConnection dbConn, string
sqlFilter, params object[] filterParams);
```

The rest of the `BicycleRepository` code deals with the adding and updating of a table row for a given `Bicycle` instance, as follows:

```
public void Add(Bicycle bicycle)
{
   Db.Insert(bicycle);
```

```
    bicycle.Id = (int)Db.GetLastInsertId();
  }
public Bicycle Update(Bicycle sourceBicycle)
  {
    Bicycle bicycle = Single(b => b.Id == sourceBicycle.Id);
    bicycle.Name = sourceBicycle.Name;
    bicycle.Type = sourceBicycle.Type;
    bicycle.Quantity = sourceBicycle.Quantity;
    bicycle.RentPrice = sourceBicycle.RentPrice;
    Db.Update(bicycle);
    return bicycle;
  }
```

Note the highlighted code that ensures that the `Id` property is set to the new database primary key value. The rest of the code is self-explanatory, and the changes made to support database persistence have left the `BicyclesService` code pretty much unchanged, apart from a refactoring that ensures that all of the data access code is delegated to `BicycleRepository`.

# Summary

In this chapter, we added the ASP.NET MVC framework to the main sample application and explored the integration points with ServiceStack and AngularJS. The bundling and minification of client-side resources was introduced, followed by a section on securing the AngularJS application and its access to web services. Various techniques to improve interaction between the frontend and backend were also introduced, and the chapter was finished off with instructions on how to add database persistence to the main sample applications using SQLite and ServiceStack.

In the next chapter, we will explore how to implement tests for AngularJS and ServiceStack and learn about support for older browsers such as Internet Explorer 8 and 9.

# 5

# Testing and Debugging AngularJS Applications

The previous chapter put together all the pieces required to build an application with AngularJS, ASP.NET MVC, and ServiceStack. In this chapter, you will explore the different aspects of testing AngularJS applications in the context of Visual Studio. We will discuss the following topics:

- Unit testing AngularJS components

- Testing an AngularJS application end to end

- Testing web service endpoints

- Unit testing .NET code

- Techniques to debug AngularJS applications

- Support for HTML5 validation and older browsers such as Internet Explorer 8 and 9

This chapter assumes you have some knowledge of testing .NET applications.

The examples in this chapter can also be found in a source control repository hosted online. Examples 1 to 7 can be found at `http://github.com/popalexandruvasile/rentthatbike` as branches of the repository (`chapter5-example1` to `chapter5-example7`).

# Overview of testing AngularJS applications

Up until this chapter, the examples we explored were concentrated on concepts, on a rapid method to prototype AngularJS applications, and on how to configure and integrate different web frameworks and application layers. As one of the goals of this book is to guide you towards building a production-ready application, we need to discuss the important topic of testing web applications. Having tests that exercise the application code thoroughly is now an essential quality of the application. This quality has the same importance as qualities like usability, maintainability, and overall performance.

Gradually, over the last decade, the subject of testing has moved to the forefront of the web application development process and all major web frameworks treat testing like a first-class citizen. Building any production-ready application needs to address testing from the beginning and adopt a testing strategy appropriate to the context in which the application is built. Retrofitting tests and ensuring the application components are testable just before the code is ready to be delivered would be a painful and costly exercise.

AngularJS was designed from the start as a framework that is easy to test. From its Version 1.0 release onwards, most of the documentation examples on http:// angularjs.org include tests alongside the example code. These tests rely on test runners developed by the AngularJS team that leverage the AngularJS framework capabilities. The test runners have evolved throughout various releases and name changes into the following test runners:

- **Karma**: This is a test runner for running unit tests. Unit tests focus on a single AngularJS component such as a service or a directive and they use fake (also called mock) dependencies injected in the component being tested. Karma can run any kind of JavaScript unit tests and can be used with non-AngularJS applications.

- **Protractor**: This is a test runner for running end-to-end tests or tests that exercise the full application using browser automation. Browser automation is provided through Selenium WebDriver. End-to-end tests are a great tool to exercise the application in a similar way with a real user.

# Introducing Node.js

We mentioned in *Chapter 2, Creating an AngularJS Client-side Application in Visual Studio*, how AngularJS documentation and examples use Node.js for building the sample code and applications. We took a different approach and used Visual Studio to install and manage AngularJS libraries and establish a .NET-based development workflow that can be used to integrate with the existing applications and libraries.

With regard to testing, the AngularJS team made a substantial investment in tools and libraries based on Node.js. The AngularJS test runners, the test configuration, and the actual tests need Node.js to be able to run. We need to introduce Node.js and explore its required tools so we can implement effective testing for AngularJS. Before doing this, I need to let you know that we will still use Visual Studio throughout this chapter thanks to the Node.js Tools for Visual Studio project available at `http://nodejstools.codeplex.com`. This Microsoft-led project brings support for Node.js runtime and tools to Visual Studio, and it is built with developer community contributions.

Node.js is a software runtime for building server-side applications using JavaScript. Internally, it uses the Google V8 JavaScript engine that powers the Google Chrome web browser to compile JavaScript code to native code. It is based on an asynchronous event-driven programming model with non-blocking I/O operations using a single thread of execution. This makes it a great fit for real-time applications and high-throughput web applications. Node.js benefits from all the optimizations and performance improvements that Google Chrome has introduced since its first version and it runs on all major operating systems, Linux, Mac OS X, and Windows, thanks to Microsoft contributions.

The Node.js installation comes with a built-in package manager called npm that is very similar to the NuGet package manager we introduced in *Chapter 2, Creating an AngularJS Client-side Application in Visual Studio*. There is an online npm package repository available at `www.npmjs.org` that is used for installing or updating Node.js application dependencies. All AngularJS test runners and associated tools are provided as npm packages, and the npm package manager is included in every Node.js installation. In this chapter, we will focus only on the Node.js features that allow us to execute AngularJS tests. Node.js development in general is outside of the scope of this book, but you can explore more about Node.js at `http://nodejs.org`.

# Setting up the Node.js environment

To set up the Node.js environment, we firstly need to install Node.js, which comes in 32-bit and 64-bit versions. Go to `http://nodejs.org/dist/v0.10.28/node-v0.10.28-x86.msi` for the 32-bit version or `http://nodejs.org/dist/v0.10.28/x64/node-v0.10.28-x64.msi` for the 64-bit version. We will install the 32-bit version. To verify that it has installed correctly, we need to open a Windows command prompt and execute the following command:

```
node -v
```

If you see **v0.10.28** on the screen, it means that Node.js has installed correctly. You might need to restart Windows if you have any problems with this command. The next step is to install Node.js Tools for Visual Studio, which is available at `http://nodejstools.codeplex.com`; at the time of this writing, there was a 1.0 Beta Version available for download at `https://nodejstools.codeplex.com/releases`.

> When you read this book, you might find that Node.js Tools for Visual Studio is released officially with a 1.0 Version. All the examples should work fine with this released version, and I would recommend that you use this one if it is available rather than the 1.0 Beta Version.
>
> Node.js Tools for Visual Studio are also available for the free Visual Studio 2013 Express for Web version, which means that none of the code examples of this book require a Visual Studio license to be purchased.

This version brings Node.js and npm integration to Visual Studio, and after it is installed you will see new options to create Node.js projects, as shown in the following screenshot:

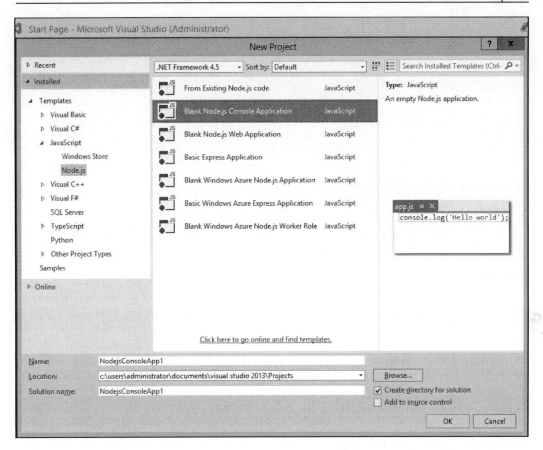

If we select the **Blank Node.js Console Application** option and create a new project, we now have a base project that we can start using to implement AngularJS tests.

By using Visual Studio to execute and debug Node.js projects, you can leverage the existing functionality, for example, Intellisense, code completion, and inspecting local variables in the **Locals** window. You can also execute arbitrary code in the **Immediate** window, break on specific Node.js exceptions with the **Exceptions** window, and even use **Edit and continue** capabilities. You can find more about these features and many others at `http://nodejstools.codeplex.com/documentation`. The following screenshot shows a sample debugging session:

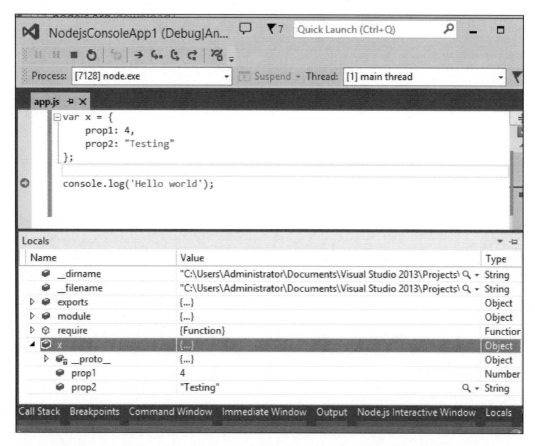

# Unit testing AngularJS components

We mentioned Karma before, the test runner for unit tests. This is the primary tool to run tests that target specific AngularJS components. We can add it to our application by creating a Node.js console project and then use npm to install the required packages.

Karma can also run generic JavaScript tests and be used as a very fast non-AngularJS test runner. More details can be found at `http://karma-runner.github.io`.

# Installing Karma

To install Karma, we first need to create a blank Node.js console application. The name I used for the main sample application AngularJS test project was `RentThatBike.Tests.Nodejs`. A `package.json` file was created for us in this project that contains metadata information such as project name, description, and author name, along with a list of npm packages that the project is using. This file is used by npm to install missing packages or update existing packages that the current project depends upon. There is a distinction being made between packages required for production, enumerated in the `dependencies` property, and the ones required for development, which are present in the `devDependencies` property. The packages required for this chapter are development packages: they deal with testing concerns and nothing else.

Although Node.js Tools for Visual Studio has user interface support for installing and managing npm packages, we will take a similar approach with NuGet and use the command line. To get access to a convenient way to launch the command line for Node.js, we need to install the Productivity Power Tools 2013 extension for Visual Studio, available at `http://visualstudiogallery.msdn.microsoft.com/dbcb8670-889e-4a54-a226-a48a15e4cace`. With this extension installed, we can now right-click on the test project node in **Solution Explorer** and navigate to **Power Commands | Open Command Prompt** and a new command window should open with the current path set to the test project path.

 If you are using Visual Studio 2013 Express for Web, you cannot install this extension and you need to open a command window and execute the commands mentioned as follows with the current path set to the test project path.

To install Karma and related packages, we need to run the following npm commands:

```
npm install karma --save-dev
npm install karma-jasmine karma-chrome-launcher --save-dev
```

The `--save-dev` switch will ensure these packages are installed as development dependencies. The first command installs the actual test runner. The second command installs multiple packages at once: the first package is the Karma adapter for Jasmine (a JavaScript testing library) and the second one will allow Karma to run tests using the Google Chrome browser (this browser also needs to be installed if not present). These packages will be installed in a `node_modules` folder in the current project and they will also be displayed under the `npm` project node in the Visual Studio **Solution Explorer** window.

There are some packages that can be installed in the Node.js installation folder and they will have a global scope (available in the command line for any path). One such package allows us to execute Karma directly without specifying its location from any Node.js project that has a Karma package installed. The following command installs the package; note the `-g` argument, which ensures the package has a global scope by installing it under the path `%USERPROFILE%\AppData\Roaming\npm`:

```
npm install -g karma-cli
```

# Configuring Karma

The next step is to create a Karma configuration file that will be used to locate the tests, execute them against the desired browsers, and generate the test output. Within the same command window, you need to execute the following command line:

```
karma init karma.conf.js
```

A series of questions will follow next in the command window, and we will accept all the default answers by pressing *ENTER* multiple times. The first question is about the testing framework to be used and it defaults to **Jasmine**, the second is if we use Require.js and the default answer is **no**, the third is about the browser used to run the tests and it defaults to **Chrome**. The fourth and fifth questions are about test file inclusions and exclusions, and the default values do not specify any files. The final question is about whether we want to run the test each time a file is changed; we will leave the default option as it is, which is **yes**.

The file we just created defines the Karma configuration object and it needs to be included in the current Visual Studio Node.js project. The next change required for this file is to add test file locations as an array for the `files` property, as shown in the following code:

```
files: [
  //external files
    '../RentThatBike.Web/scripts/angular.js',
    '../RentThatBike.Web/scripts/angular-mocks.js',
    '../RentThatBike.Web/scripts/angular-route.js',
    '../RentThatBike.Web/scripts/angular-resource.js',
    '../RentThatBike.Web/scripts/angular-spinner.js',
    '../RentThatBike.Web/scripts/ui-bootstrap-*.js',

  //App code
    '../RentThatBike.Web/scripts/app/**/*.js',

  //Tests
  'tests/unit/**/*Spec.js'
],
```

Because Karma needs to run tests for AngularJS components, we have included all AngularJS and JavaScript libraries from the web application project first followed by the application-specific files using a recursive file selection pattern. We also included the `angular-mocks.js` file, which will be used during testing. The last file pattern is reserved for the actual unit test files that we need to define next. The order of the script references from this file is important as we are loading the JavaScript resources from the `_Layout.cshtml` file and we need to preserve their original position.

# Creating AngularJS unit tests with Jasmine

In the current configuration, Karma will use Jasmine to define the tests. Jasmine is a **Behavior-Driven Development (BDD)** framework that contains extensive built-in functionality to define and execute tests for JavaScript code. A BDD framework differs from traditional test frameworks like MSTest and NUnit because it defines tests as a desired behavior, where the test outcome is specified first, followed by the actual test assertion. Jasmine uses a `describe/it` syntax to define test specification while other BDD frameworks use a `given/when/then` syntax, which will be covered in the .NET testing section later on in this chapter.

# Jasmine essentials

A typical Jasmine test that asserts the result of a trivial JavaScript operation will have the following code (with the Jasmine-specific functions highlighted):

```
describe("A basic Javascript add operation", function() {
  it("should be correct", function() {
    var result = 1 + 1;
    expect(result).toEqual(2);
  });
});
```

When running the test, its output should read **A basic JavaScript add operation should be correct**, forming a meaningful statement about the value delivered by the code under test. The `describe` call is a Jasmine global function that will group one or more test specifications that are defined by the `it` function (which is also another Jasmine global function). Both functions have a test-related description as the first argument. The second argument is a function that defines the test suite in its body with the test specification (or the spec) defined in the `it` function. Test assertions use the Jasmine global function `expect`, which is chained with a helper function called **matcher** that will facilitate the test result evaluation. There are a couple of built-in **matcher** functions available, such as `toBe`, which checks if the test assertion object and the expected object are the same; `toEqual`, which checks if the two objects are equivalent; and `toBeDefined`, which checks that the test assertion object is not undefined. You can also define your own custom matchers for more complex expectation checks. Jasmine allows you to set up and tear down data before and after a spec is executed through the global functions `beforeEach` and `afterEach`. We will explore some of the Jasmine features mentioned here in the upcoming tests of this chapter.

 More information about all available matcher functions and more features like test doubles for the default version of Jasmine provided with Karma can be found at http://jasmine.github.io/1.3/introduction.html.

# Using the ngMock module for the first test

We can now proceed and implement the first test for our AngularJS application by creating a test file for the `bicyclesController` component at the location specified in the Karma configuration file and named accordingly, `tests\unit\controllers\bicyclesControllerSpec.js`. The following code is the content of this file:

```
'use strict';
describe("bicyclesController", function () {
    beforeEach(module('myApp'));
    it('should be defined', inject(function ($controller) {
        var bicyclesController = $controller('BicyclesController',
{ $scope: {} });
        expect(bicyclesController).toBeDefined();
    }));
});
```

Note the first highlighted function, which is a global function defined in the `angular-mocks.js` file. This function is a convenient shortcut to the `angular.mock.module` function that loads our AngularJS application module and implicitly the ngMock module from the `angular-mocks.js` file in preparation for unit testing. The ngMock module contains the required functionality to test AngularJS components. By loading our application module in this way, we prepare it for integration with the ngMock module and we have some of the built-in AngularJS components replaced with test-friendly alternatives. For example, our services depend on the ngResource module, which in turn depends on the low-level `$http` service, which also depends on the `$httpBackend` service. The `$httpBackend` service is tasked with making the actual request for data from the remote server, and it will be replaced with a fake `$httpBackend` service when we use the `angular.mock.module` function. Whenever a data request is triggered, the fake `$httpBackend` service will ensure that a remote call is avoided. This replacement service provides extra functionality to simulate the remote server responses, to verify that specific requests were made, and to flush requests as if they were accepted and resolved by the remote server.

The next highlighted function `inject` is also a global function that is a shortcut to the `angular.mock.inject` function provided by the ngMock module. This function gives us access to the dependency injection infrastructure, and we can modify or extract any application component for test-related manipulation. In the example above, we were able to get access to the `$controller` service and create a `BicyclesController` component that has a custom `$scope` instance. The test simply asserts that the specific controller instance can be created and it covers the scenario when the controller under test is renamed or deleted inadvertently.

You can explore this test in the `Example1` folder from the source code of this chapter. There is a new solution file, `RentThatBike_With_Nodejs.sln`, that you can use if Node.js Tools for Visual Studio is installed. The Karma configuration for this example uses an additional test reporter provided by the karma-xml-reporter npm package. This reporter will convert the test results to a Visual-Studio-friendly format. If the Visual Studio extension VS Adapter for Google's Karma test runner is installed and the Visual Studio menu option under **TEST | Test Settings | Run Tests After Build** is enabled, the Karma test results will be displayed in the Visual Studio **Test Explorer** window. The following screenshot shows how what test result from the previous example looks like in Visual Studio when using this extension:

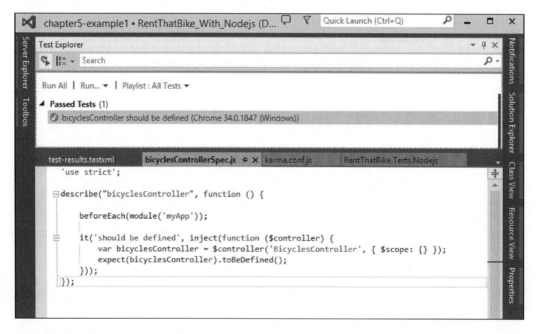

You can also run Karma tests from the Node.js test project command window by executing the following command:

```
karma start karma.conf.js
```

# Mocking remote server calls with $httpBackend

There are controller tests where you want to ensure that any remote data is provided in a predictable manner so it can be used in assertions. We will implement a test for the `BicyclesController` component that will rely on remote data being injected with specific values. To do that, we can either mock the `bicyclesService` component directly or we can use the `$httpBackend` service to provide the data returned by `bicyclesService` to our controller. Usually, the first approach is suitable when the controller has significant application logic and we want to completely isolate the controller code from its dependencies. Because in our example the controller just calls the service, I have added a new spec that showcases the latter approach, as shown in the following code:

```
it('should have 2 bicycles', inject(function ($httpBackend,
$controller) {
  $httpBackend.expectGET('api/bicycles')
        .respond(200, [{ id: 1, name: 'testBicycle1' },
                    { id: 2, name: 'testBicycle2' }]);
  var $scope = {};
  $controller('BicyclesController', { $scope: $scope });
  $httpBackend.flush();
  expect($scope.bicycles).toBeDefined();
  expect($scope.bicycles.length).toEqual(2);
  expect($scope.bicycles[1].name).toEqual("testBicycle2");
  $httpBackend.verifyNoOutstandingExpectation();
  $httpBackend.verifyNoOutstandingRequest();
}));
```

As in the previous example, we used the `inject` function to get access to the `$httpBackend` service. This service is the fake version provided in the ngMock module so we can use its helper methods to simulate remote data responses. The first highlighted function `expectGET` will set up an expectation that a request for a specific route is made. There are several similar helper methods available, such as `$httpBackend.expectPOST`, which will work with any HTTP verb available and any route. The second highlighted function, `respond`, will return a specific response with a predefined HTTP status code and data when the expected route is hit.

The third highlighted function, `flush`, will ensure the response from the remote server is simulated and all issued requests are fulfilled. The response data that we supplied will be returned only when the `$httpBackend.flush()` method is called. This method resolves all pending promises created for the simulated remote data calls.

The last highlighted functions, `verifyNoOutstandingExpectation` and `verifyNoOutstandingRequest`, are meant to perform a safety check and ensure that all `$httpBackend` service expectations are met.

You can explore the tests for this section in the `Example2` folder of the source code for this chapter. There is also a `bicycleControllerSpec.js` file that contains similar tests for the `BicycleController` component that has more logic, and it uses the promises functionality.

# Testing an AngularJS application end to end

AngularJS has a great story for implementing end-to-end tests that verify user interaction with the web application under test through the browser client. The test runner that facilitates these tests is Protractor, which is an AngularJS-friendly wrapper around the Selenium WebDriver browser automation framework. Selenium WebDriver can issue commands against a specific browser and retrieve the results, allowing test frameworks to set up test scenarios and make assertions against the actual content rendered in the browser. Protractor has access to the Selenium WebDriver API through a set of JavaScript bindings called WebDriverJS, and by default will use a Node.js version of Jasmine to define the tests. Protractor wraps the functionality offered by WebDriverJS, offering a different API that is AngularJS-aware and will only work for web pages that are AngularJS applications. You can still access original WebDriverJS functionality when working with pages that don't have AngularJS included, such as the login page from our main sample application.

## Installing Protractor

Before we install Protractor, we need to ensure the Selenium WebDriver is installed. Its core implementation is done in Java, so it requires the **Java Development Kit (JDK)** to be installed as a prerequisite. The JDK is available at www.oracle.com/technetwork/java/javase/downloads/index.html.

To verify that the JDK is installed, you need to run the following command successfully:

```
java -version
```

After this step, we can go back to our Node.js test project and use npm in the project command window to install Protractor as a development dependency, as shown in the following code:

```
npm install protractor -save-dev
```

Protractor includes the selenium-webdriver npm package that we can now use to install the Selenium WebDriver server and its Google-Chrome-specific integration, provided by the ChromeDriver library, using the following command:

```
node_modules\.bin\webdriver-manager update
```

The Selenium WebDriver server is required if we want to run tests against different browsers apart from Google Chrome, and it needs to be started before we run any tests in its own project command window by executing the following command:

```
node_modules\.bin\webdriver-manager start
```

 You can find out more about Protractor browser support at `http://github.com/angular/protractor/blob/master/docs/browser-setup.md`.

# Configuring Protractor

Protractor needs a configuration file to run tests, and this file needs to be created manually. The file is similar to the Karma configuration file and the following code shows the version used for our sample application:

```
exports.config = {
    seleniumAddress: 'http://localhost:4444/wd/hub',
    capabilities: {
        'browserName': 'chrome',
        'chromeOptions': {
            'args': ['window-size=1024,768']
        }
    },
    specs: ['tests/e2e/**/*Spec.js'],
    jasmineNodeOpts: {
        showColors: true, // Use colors in the command line
report.
    }
};
```

The `seleniumAddress` value is the default Selenium WebDriver server endpoint where browser automation commands will be sent. The `capabilities` property specifies the browser used for end-to-end testing, which is Google Chrome in our example, and this property will be passed to the Selenium WebDriver server. It also sets the browser window size that will be used during testing. The `specs` property specifies one or more files or file patterns that contain the tests, and the last property will configure Jasmine options.

We can now check that the configuration is correct by running the following command in the project command window:

```
node_modules\.bin\protractor protractor.conf.js
```

Even if there are no tests defined, the command should be successful, with a **0 tests** message displayed.

# Writing Protractor tests

We can now write the first end-to-end tests that will target the **Bicycles** application page. The test will load the browser page and then identify specific HTML elements and execute assertions against them. As the test will load the browser page as a real user would, we need to ensure the login page is processed first.

Because we use Jasmine, the tests' structure is the same as the Karma tests we explored earlier. We will implement a `beforeEach` call tasked with bypassing the login page and loading the **Bicycles** page, as shown in the following code:

```
describe('Bicycles page', function () {
    beforeEach(function () {
        var ptor = protractor.getInstance();
        var driver = ptor.driver;
        driver.get('http://localhost:61803/');

        var loginButton =
driver.findElement(protractor.By.className('btn'));
        loginButton.click();

        browser.get('http://localhost:61803/#/bicycles');
    });
});
```

As the Protractor API works only for AngularJS pages and our login page does not have any AngularJS references, we need to use the original WebDriver API first. The WebDriver API can be called through the `ptor.driver` property of the Protractor singleton instance obtained by executing the function `protractor.getInstance()`. Calling the WebDriver `findElement` function and using the WebDriver built-in element locator provided through the `protractor.By` property ensures the page login button is clicked on and we are redirected to the AngularJS application home page. We don't need to specify the username and password explicitly as the ASP. NET MVC application will fill them in for us.

From this point on, we can use the Protractor API, which is simpler and has built-in selectors that leverage AngularJS. First we load the desired page through the `browser` global property and then we will use a Protractor locator to get the HTML element that has the page title to assert the first test condition, as shown in the following code:

```
it('should display the correct title', function () {
  var title = element(by.css('.col-md-12 h1'));
  expect(title.getText()).toEqual('Bicycles');
});
```

Note how the Protractor locator is similar to the WebDriver locator and moreover has a slightly more concise and expressive API. The following test case shows an AngularJS-specific locator that we can use to locate an element by its binding property:

```
it('should display the logged on user details', function () {
  var displayName =
element(by.binding('serverSideData.userDisplayName'));
  expect(displayName.getText()).toEqual('Admin
User(admin@rentthatbike.com)');
});
```

Protractor shows its power when we use specific scope properties to locate elements, making the tests less subjective to change compared to regular WebDriver tests. The markup can change significantly between test runs, but you will still be able to reference the scope properties as long as their names don't change.

The final test shows how we can select multiple elements rendered by an `ngRepeat` directive using just a special locator based on the `ngRepeat` directive expression, as shown in the following code:

```
it('should display 4 bicycles', function () {
  var bicycles = element.all(by.repeater('bicycle in bicycles'));
  expect(bicycles.count()).toEqual(4);
});
```

Again, this shows that the focus of the Protractor tests is on the AngularJS scope properties and the semantic structure of the page rather than the specific HTML that gets rendered on the page. You can find these tests in the `Example3` folder from the source code of this chapter.

 Protractor uses a modified version of Jasmine with an `expect()` implementation that will resolve the promise returned by a Protractor locator such as `element.all()` before verifying the test assertion.

# Testing web service endpoints

Testing server-side components is a key ingredient for building a solid AngularJS application. All web service endpoints should be exercised through tests as they have a relatively low cost in configuration and implementation when using ServiceStack. Because all the core functionality of the application is provided by ServiceStack web services, we will focus on testing these rather than the ASP.NET MVC controllers. You can cover the little functionality provided by ASP.NET MVC in end-to-end tests executed by Protractor.

We will change the strategy here and rather than start exploring unit tests, we will look at endpoint tests first. This is an outside-in test strategy that can also be extended to AngularJS tests depending on your preferred workflow. You can start with Protractor tests as they are the highest level tests, then move to Karma-based tests, and then continue with web services endpoint tests as described in this section. The web service endpoint tests can be viewed as end-to-end tests where the user that drives the tests is a web service client rather than a browser user.

# Configuring self-hosted ServiceStack web services

We will create a new C# library project in Visual Studio to host the tests; I called this project RentThatBike.Tests for our main sample solution. Next, we will define a new ServiceStack web services host that reuses most of the web application configuration and it will run the tests. The difference from the existing host is that the test-specific ServiceStack host will run in a self-hosted process rather than using IIS. First of all, we need to add the ServiceStack and ServiceStack.OrmLite.Sqlite32 NuGet packages to the new test project using the following commands:

```
Install-Package ServiceStack -Version 3.9.71 -DependencyVersion
Highest
```

```
Install-Package ServiceStack.OrmLite.Sqlite32 -Version 3.9.71
```

Then we will go back to the RentThatBike.Web project and extract the ServiceStack configuration code from the AppHost class into a new AppHostConfiguration class that we will be able to reuse later. The following code shows what the AppHost. Configure method looks like now:

```
public override void Configure(Container container)
{
  //ASP.NET MVC integration
  ControllerBuilder.Current.SetControllerFactory(new
FunqControllerFactory(container));
  SetConfig(CreateEndpointHostConfig());
  var appHostConfiguration = new AppHostConfiguration(this);
  appHostConfiguration.ConfigureAppHost(container);
}
```

Rather than passing the AppHost type to AppHostConfiguration, we can use the IAppHost interface provided by ServiceStack as it is implemented by the ServiceStack ASP.NET host implementation (AppHostBase) and the self-hosted one (AppHostHttpListenerBase). IAppHost contains all the properties and methods that are needed. We can now implement the self-hosted version of the AppHost class in the test project as shown in the following code:

```
public class AppHostTest : AppHostHttpListenerBase
{
  public AppHostTest()
```

```
        : base("Rent That Bike! Web services Test",
typeof(AppHost).Assembly)
  {
  }
  public override void Configure(Container container)
  {
      SetConfig(CreateEndpointHostConfig());
      var appHostConfiguration = new
AppHostConfiguration(this);
      appHostConfiguration.ConfigureAppHost(container,
useTestDatabase: true);
  }
  private EndpointHostConfig CreateEndpointHostConfig()
  {
      return new EndpointHostConfig
      {
          DebugMode = true,
          DefaultContentType = ContentType.Json,
      };
  }
}
```

Because ServiceStack is now self-hosted and is not using the ASP.NET platform, we don't need to set the `IControllerFactory` instance for ASP.NET MVC. The test web services address is using the application host address directly rather than the relative `api` path as you can see in the `EndpointHostConfig` definition. I have chosen this particular configuration to showcase how flexible the web services host is and how easy it is to set up ServiceStack to run independently from ASP.NET MVC while retaining all the functionality implemented in the previous chapter.

The highlighted parameter in the `appHostConfiguration.ConfigureAppHost` call will initialize the SQLite database to run in memory rather than using a file saved to disk. The following code shows how the `IDbConnectionFactory` interface is registered now:

```
if (useTestDatabase)
{
  container.Register<IDbConnectionFactory>(
      new OrmLiteConnectionFactory(
          ":memory:",
          false,
          SqliteDialect.Provider));
}
else
{
```

```
container.Register<IDbConnectionFactory>(
    new OrmLiteConnectionFactory(
        ConfigurationManager.ConnectionStrings["SqlLiteConnection"].
Connec
tionString.MapHostAbsolutePath(),
        SqliteDialect.Provider));
}
```

Note the database configuration string in the highlighted code snippet. This sets SQLite in a mode of operation where all database queries run in memory and are not persisted to a database file. Because of this mode of operation, we also need to specify the next parameter, called `autoDisposeConnection`, to ensure the database connection remains open throughout testing. Otherwise, we could lose data inserted for tests when the database connection is closed and reopened.

This configuration should speed up our tests considerably while exercising the data persistence layer thoroughly.

# Adding BDD tests with xBehave.net

With the test web services configuration out of the way, we can now proceed and write our first tests. When writing .NET-based tests, we can use a rich variety of classic testing frameworks (also known as TDD frameworks) such as MSTest, NUnit, and xUnit.net, or we can use BDD frameworks such as NSpec, SpecFlow, and xBehave.net to name just a few. We will maintain the testing style of the AngularJS applications and use a BDD framework that allows us to write tests as specifications in an easy-to-read format.

When writing end-to-end tests, you usually want to meet the acceptance criteria agreed upon with the project stakeholders. These types of test are usually described in a common language that can be easily read by non-developers. For example, if our web services are exposed to third-party clients, we can use the following sentence to describe the functionality provided by a web service method:

> *Given the seed data is created, when a GET bicycles request is made using admin credentials, then the response is not null and 4 bicycles are returned.*

The language might appear a bit technical, but it can be understood easily and it follows a `given`/`when`/`then` (GWT) syntax that helps in breaking the specification into distinct steps. The GWT syntax is popular in BDD frameworks like Cucumber for Ruby and SpecFlow or xBehave.net for .NET.

We will use a simple yet powerful BDD framework called xBehave.net to implement our tests using the GWT syntax. This framework relies on another great test framework called xUnit.net for its implementation. The xUnit.net framework has one of the original authors of NUnit among its contributors and it aims to provide simpler test syntax support while being very extensible; these are just a few of its features. It allows developers to easily define their own syntax when implementing tests, and because of that, it has become a favorite base library for other test frameworks like xBehave.net.

An empty test using xBehave.net will have the following code:

```
public class BicyclesServiceSpecs
{
  [Scenario]
  public void GetBicyclesWithSeedData()
  {
      "Given the seed data is created"
          .Given(() => { });
      "When a GET bicycles request is made using admin credentials"
          .When(() => {});
      "Then the response is not null."
          .Then(() => {});

      "And 4 bicycles are returned."
          .Then(() => {});
  }
}
```

Note the relatively small amount of code we need to write to transition from the specification text to a ready-to-implement test suite using the highlighted methods. These methods are implemented as extension methods for the `string` type, which gives us an expressive and fluent way to define the tests. The test method is marked by the xBehave.net `Scenario` attribute, which is derived from the xUnit.net `Fact` attribute that also marks xUnit.net test methods. This makes the tooling built for xUnit.net tests also recognize xBehave.net tests using Visual Studio or the command line.

To add xBehave.net to our test project, we need to run the following NuGet Package Manager Console command:

```
Install-Package Xbehave -Version 1.1.0
```

We can now implement the body of the `GetBicyclesWithSeedData` test method as shown in the following code:

```
List<Bicycle> bicycles = null;
"Given the seed data is created"
  .Given(() => { });
"When a GET bicycles request is made using admin credentials"
  .When(() =>
  {
      var restClient = new JsonServiceClient(BaseUrl);
      restClient.Send(new Auth
      {
          provider = CredentialsAuthProvider.Name,
          UserName = "admin@rentthatbike.com",
          Password = "admin",
          RememberMe = true,
      });
      bicycles = restClient.Get(new GetBicycles());
  });
"Then the response is not null."
  .Then(() => { Assert.NotNull(bicycles); });
"And 4 bicycles are returned."
  .Then(() => { Assert.Equal(4, bicycles.Count); });
```

The `Given` step is empty for this test as there is no other test preparation apart from the seed data that is already created when the application starts. The `When` method contains the actual web service call and it will authenticate the test user as a prerequisite for the data request. We have two test assertions that are performed in separate `Then` method calls using the xUnit.net assertion methods `Assert.NotNull` and `Assert.Equal`.

 The test assertions provided by xUnit.net are focused on simplicity but you can replace these by using more expressive test assertion libraries such as Fluent Assertions, which is available at `http://github.com/dennisdoomen/FluentAssertions`.

The default behavior of xBehave.net is to mark all the test steps as failed after the first test step fails so we will be able to identify the failing step just by reading the test output.

To execute the tests, you can either install the Visual Studio extension xUnit.net runner for Visual Studio 2012 and 2013 available at `http://visualstudiogallery.msdn.microsoft.com/463c5987-f82b-46c8-a97e-b1cde42b9099` or use the xUnit.net test runner from the NuGet package, which can be installed with the following command:

```
Install-Package xunit.runners -Version 1.9.2
```

The Visual Studio extension will make the tests discoverable in the **Test Explorer** window and the xUnit.net console runner can be executed in the test project command window using the following command line:

```
..\packages\xunit.runners.1.9.2\tools\xunit.console.clr4.x86.exe
bin\Debug\RentThatBike.Tests.dll
```

You can explore the tests in the `Example4` folder from the source code of this chapter. The Visual Studio build configuration for the solution needs to be set to the `x86` platform because we are using the SQLite 32-bit version.

For convenience, we initialized the ServiceStack application host in the static constructor of the test class so that when the tests run the web services' infrastructure is already available.

# Unit testing .NET code

We can use the same BDD syntax introduced in the previous section when implementing unit tests, but sometimes using a classic test syntax will be more suitable for smaller and more focused tests. Let's take the `Bicycle` class and imagine a simple test that verifies the functionality provided by the `TypeName` property using xUnit.net and the TDD syntax, as shown in the following code:

```
public class BicycleTests
{
  [Fact]
  public void TypeNameIsFormatted()
  {
      var bicycle = new Bicycle
      {
          Type = BicycleTypes.MountainBike
      };
      Assert.Equal("Mountain Bike", bicycle.TypeName);
  }
}
```

Note the `Fact` attribute that marks the test method and the `Assert.Equal` call that will verify the expected result.

However, for more complex tests, even if they are unit tests, you may find the BDD syntax more expressive and easier to use. For example, if we want to test the `BicycleValidator` class, its specification could read something like the following sentence:

> *Given an empty bicycle instance, when it is validated, then the bicycle is not valid and it has three validation errors.*

We can now proceed to implement the test starting from this specification.

The class being tested has a dependency on the `BicycleRepository` class, which in turn depends on the database storage being configured. In this test, we only want to test the functionality of the `BicycleValidator` class, so we need to be able to pass in a `BicycleRepository` dependency that can be easily modified with data that is suitable for the test and break the database persistence dependency. To achieve this, the first step is to extract the functionality from the `BicycleRepository` dependency into an interface called `IBcycleRepository`. We can then implement the interface in a test-friendly class that is only used to provide test data. Alternatively, we can save some keystrokes and use a mocking framework and implement the interface dynamically.

A mocking framework will also help with providing data for interface functions and properties. It can verify that specific functions were called and it can also check the arguments used in interface functions calls. There are several mocking frameworks available for .NET, and the one we will use for its low footprint and versatility is called Moq.

 You can find more information about the Moq framework at `http://github.com/Moq/moq4`.

It can be installed as a NuGet package with the following command:

```
Install-Package Moq -Version 4.2.1402.2112
```

The following code shows what the test method looks like when using Moq:

```
[Scenario]
public void ValidatesIncompleteBicycle()
{
  Bicycle bicycle = null;
  ValidationResult validationResult = null;
  "Given an empty bicycle instance"
      .Given(() => { bicycle = new Bicycle(); });
  "When is validated"
      .When(() =>
      {
```

```
            IBicyleRepository bicyleRepository =
  Mock.Of<IBicyleRepository>();
            var bicycleValidator = new
  BicycleValidator(bicyleRepository);
            validationResult =
  bicycleValidator.Validate(bicycle);
        });
    "Then the bicycle is not valid"
        .Then(() => { Assert.False(validationResult.IsValid); });
    "And it has three validation errors"
        .Then(() => { Assert.Equal(3,
  validationResult.Errors.Count); });
    }
```

Note how we used only one line to create a mocked instance for
`IBicycleRepository`. Because here we are not testing all features of the
`BicycleValidator` class, the mocked instance is only used to satisfy the dependency
on `IBicycleRepository`. For other tests you can use the Moq API to instrument a
mocked instance to return specific data when its properties or functions are called by
the code being tested.

You can explore the tests from this section in the `Example5` folder from the source
code of this chapter.

# Techniques to debug AngularJS applications

When an application has comprehensive suites of tests, there is very little need for
debugging. However, for situations when debugging is required, there are some
good options that you can use.

The AngularJS team have provided a Google Chrome extension called AngularJS
Batarang that can be used to inspect and even run performance analysis for an
AngularJS application. One of the most important features is scope inspection. You
can use it, for example, to inspect the controller scope from the **Bicycles** page and
to display the scope of each repeater item from the same page, as shown in the
following screenshot:

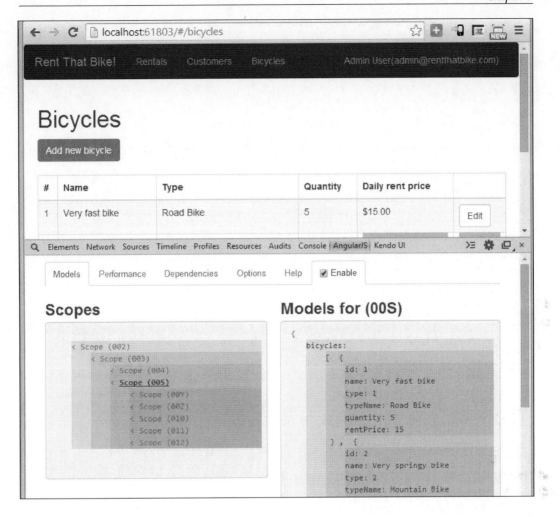

The extension has a selection tool that allows you to point to a visual element and then display the scope available for that element. More details about this extension can be found at `http://github.com/angular/angularjs-batarang`.

When writing Karma tests, you can experience test failures that might need debugging. At the time of writing this book, Node.js Tools for Visual Studio doesn't have the ability to debug Karma tests outright, but you can debug them in the browser. In the current main sample project configuration, whenever a Karma test is executed, a Google Chrome window will be launched. You can find a **DEBUG** link on the launched page that will load the Karma tests files together with all the other scripts referenced in the Karma configuration file. Using Chrome Developer Tools, you can then put breakpoints in the desired tests or view the Karma test output in the **Console** tab. You can also use Visual Studio to debug the same scripts when running Karma in Internet Explorer using the steps described at `http://nodejstools.codeplex.com/workitem/883`.

All Protractor end-to-end tests can be debugged in Visual Studio without any problems with Node.js Tools for Visual Studio by placing a breakpoint at the desired test code line. Protractor also supports an interactive debugging mode where you can inspect the page elements through WebDriver when executing the following command line in the Node.js test project command window:

```
node_modules\.bin\protractor debug protractor.conf.js
```

Pressing *c* will advance through the tests and inserting a `browser.debugger();` line in any test will cause Protractor to stop at that line during the interactive debug session. Within this session, you can access the Protractor API and inspect HTML elements with the following code:

```
element(by.id('foobar')).getText()
```

# Support for HTML5 validation and older browsers such as Internet Explorer 8 and 9

Another important step in preparing a web application for release is ensuring it supports its target browsers and renders HTML that is compliant with W3C validation rules. The examples explored so far have used minimal markup to ensure they only focus on the concepts and don't include any non-essential content. However, if we run our main application pages through an HTML5 validation tool, you will see many validation failures. This is mainly due to the fact that AngularJS uses custom HTML attributes such as `ng-app` and `ng-view` and these are not valid HTML5 markup. We need to ensure all these attributes are prefixed with `data-` or `x-` to pass validation.

The main sample application was converted to use the HTML5-compliant tags and attributes, and you can explore the changes in the `Example6` folder from the source code of this chapter. From now on, we will have HTML5-compliant markup and you can validate the application HTML using an online tool such as the one available at `http://validator.w3.org` or through a browser extension such as the Validity Google Chrome extension.

If your application needs to support older versions of Internet Explorer, there are a couple of required changes that we need to discuss. We will only address support for Internet Explorer 8 and 9 here, as anything older is not supported by AngularJS 1.2 and even Internet Explorer 8 support will be dropped in AngularJS 1.3 and above.

Internet Explorer 8 has very little support for HTML5 and CSS3, so any HTML5 tags like the ones we used in the main sample application (for example, `header` and `section`) will not be recognized or rendered properly. Internet Explorer 9 has some support for HTML5 and CSS3 but there are a lot of missing bits such as support for the `placeholder` attribute or the CSS3 `transition` feature.

Thanks to the efforts of the open source community, there is a JavaScript library called HTML5 Shiv that provides some of the missing HTML5 tags for Internet Explorer 8. This library is included in a bigger HTML5 and CSS3 feature-detection library called Modernizr. By including this library in our main sample project, we will restore some functionality to Internet Explorer 8 and provide HTML5 and CSS3 feature-detection capabilities for other partially-compliant browsers such as Internet Explorer 9.

CSS3 also introduces the media query feature, which allows conditional styling based on the current device resolution, and this is not supported in Internet Explorer 8. Another JavaScript library, called Respond.js, will enable this feature, which is heavily used by Twitter Bootstrap.

To install the NuGet packages for these libraries, you need to execute the following commands:

```
Install-Package Modernizr
Install-Package Respond
```

They are included in the `BundleConfig.cs` file in a bundle called `browser-support` that is imported in the `head` section of the `_Layout.cshtml` page. This will ensure the HTML not supported by Internet Explorer 8 will be provided as soon as the page is loaded and any CSS relying on media queries will look correct when the page is rendered. This is how the start of the `_Layout.cshtml` page looks now:

```
<!DOCTYPE HTML>
<html id="ng-app" data-ng-app="myApp">
```

```
<head>
  <!--[if lte IE 8]>
    <script>
      document.createElement('ng-include');
      document.createElement('ng-pluralize');
      document.createElement('ng-view');

      // Optionally these for CSS
      document.createElement('ng:include');
      document.createElement('ng:pluralize');
      document.createElement('ng:view');
    </script>
  <![endif]-->
  <meta charset="utf-8" />
  <meta http-equiv="X-UA-Compatible" content="IE=edge">
  <title>@ViewBag.Title</title>
  @Styles.Render("~/Content/css")
  @Scripts.Render("~/bundles/browser-support")
</head>
```

The highlighted code is Internet-Explorer-specific markup that also needs to be included for Internet Explorer 8 support. You can explore these changes in the Example7 folder from the source code of this chapter.

 The application should be very easy to adapt for responsive web design requirements due to Twitter Bootstrap's built-in features. This is where Modernizr will shine as it will give you a programmatic way to adapt to various mobile browser versions.

# Summary

This chapter explored how to set up and implement testing for most of the client-side and server-side components. We also discussed HTML5 validation and older browser support, and this should give a good base to start building your very own production-ready application.

The next chapter will explore features that are not essential in building an application but are still useful to be aware of, such as internationalization support and using remote web services with AngularJS.

# 6

# Advanced AngularJS Topics

The previous chapters gradually introduced the building blocks required to create an AngularJS application using Visual Studio and .NET. In this chapter, we will go a bit further and explore the following advanced AngularJS topics:

- Internationalization and localization
- Using AngularJS animations
- Working with remote web services
- Template caching

The *Using AngularJS animations* section assumes that the reader knows the fundamentals of CSS3 transitions and animations and CSS3 vendor prefixes. The *Working with remote web services* section assumes that the reader is familiar with the structure of a **Uniform Resource Identifier (URI)**.

The *Working with remote web services* section also assumes that the reader is familiar with the XMLHttpRequest API and the HTTP request and response fundamentals.

Examples from this chapter can also be found as source control repositories hosted online. Examples 1 to 6 can be found at `https://github.com/popalexandruvasile/rentthatbike/` as branches of the main repository (`chapter6-example1` to `chapter6-example6`).

# Internationalization and localization

The building of applications often involves making them available for users from all over the world. The effort required to support this scenario is generically known as **internationalization (i18n)**. Usually, a considerable development effort is needed to implement i18n, especially when it needs to be retrofitted to an existing application. When implementing i18n, we need to address certain difficult problems, such as the following:

- Support for right-to-left languages, such as Hebrew or Arabic
- User interface resources that might not fit in the application layout, such as button labels that exceed the button's width
- Different time zones and date and number formats
- Currencies that have significant differences in their exchange rates when converted

Once i18n support is available, the application should easily support regional differences, even for the same language, or differences between languages; this effort is known as **localization (l10n)**.

# Using the ngLocale module

AngularJS has i18n and l10n support for its date, number, and currency filters, and the `ngPluralize` directive. There is an optional `ngLocale` module that is implemented in separate files, one for each distinct language code and country code combination. This combination is also known as locale ID, and valid identifiers are `en` for the default English locale or `en-gb` for the British English locale. An AngularJS application can only use one locale at a time with the `ngLocale` module, and the locale ID cannot be changed during application runtime.

To use the `ngLocale` module in our application, we need to import this NuGet package in the main sample web application project with the following command:

```
Install-Package AngularJS.Locale -Version 1.2.15
```

After the package has been installed, there will be a new `i18n` folder inside the `scripts` folder that contains the files for all supported locale identifiers. For example, if our application needs to use the `fr-fr` locale, we just need to include the `angular-locale_fr-fr.js` file in the `angular` script bundle. I added a new `Created` property to the `Bicycle` class; it will store the date and time for when a new instance was created. This property uses the date filter on the **Bicycles** and **Update bicycle** pages, and it showcases the change to the new locale together with the `RentPrice` property that uses the currency filter for display, as shown in the following screenshot:

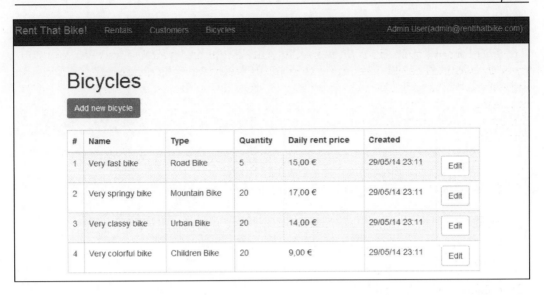

In this example, our AngularJS application will use the `fr-fr` locale ID even if the regional settings of the client browser are set to a different country or changed to a different region. You can explore the code in the `Example1` folder from the source code for this chapter.

The `ngLocale` module works well if we only plan to support a bike rental business for a specific region. What happens if we need to support customers from more than one region or country in the same application? The locale ID can be set only once, when the AngularJS application is loaded, so changing it means that we will need to restart the application, which is not an elegant or even acceptable solution. One of the workarounds suggested in the AngularJS developer guide for i18n, at `http://code.angularjs.org/1.2.15/docs/guide/i18n`, is to have separate starting pages for each supported language. We will not use this approach for our sample application; instead, we will use an alternative solution based on a new AngularJS module.

# Using the angular-dynamic-locale module

The next example will allow us to change the current locale ID dynamically using a drop-down menu that displays a list of supported locales, as shown in the following screenshot:

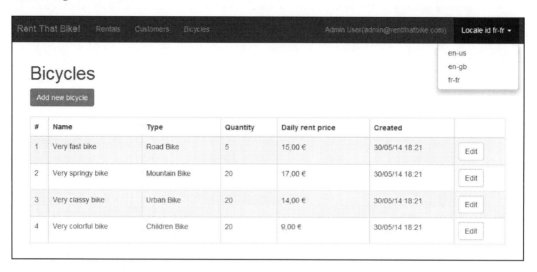

Using the module available at `https://github.com/lgalfaso/angular-dynamic-locale`, we can switch the current AngularJS locale ID dynamically. First, we need to include the `tmhDynamicLocale.js` file in the `angular` bundle in the `BundleConfig.cs` file and also import its `tmh.dynamicLocale` module in our application module. Next, we need to set the location of the AngularJS i18n path for this new module as it differs from its default value. We need to do this in our application module `config` section using the `tmhDynamicLocaleProvider` component as shown in the following code:

```
myAppModule.config(['$provide', '$httpProvider',
'tmhDynamicLocaleProvider', function ($provide, $httpProvider,
tmhDynamicLocaleProvider) {

  ...

  tmhDynamicLocaleProvider.localeLocationPattern('scripts/i18n/angul
ar-locale_{{locale}}.js');
}]);
```

With this configuration in place, we can change the application menu to include the new dropdown as shown in the following code:

```
<ul class="nav navbar-nav navbar-right">
  <li><a
href="#">{{serverSideData.userDisplayName}}({{serverSideData.userE
mail}})</a></li>
  <li class="dropdown">
      <a href="#" class="dropdown-toggle" data-
toggle="dropdown">Locale id {{selectedLocale}} <b
class="caret"></b></a>
      <ul class="dropdown-menu">
          <li data-ng-repeat="supportedLocale in
supportedLocales">
              <a href="" data-ng-
click="onLocaleChanged($index)">{{supportedLocale}}</a>
          </li>
      </ul>
  </li>
</ul>
```

Note that we only reference the `ApplicationController` scope properties, and the locale ID switch logic is executed exclusively in the controller implementation, as shown in the following code:

```
myAppModule.controller('ApplicationController', ['$scope',
'serverSideData', 'tmhDynamicLocale',
    function ($scope, serverSideData, tmhDynamicLocale) {
        ...
        $scope.supportedLocales = ['en-us', 'en-gb', 'fr-fr'];
        $scope.onLocaleChanged = function(index) {
            $scope.selectedLocale =
$scope.supportedLocales[index];
            tmhDynamicLocale.set($scope.selectedLocale);
        };
        $scope.onLocaleChanged(0);
    }
]);
```

We arbitrarily support only three locale IDs, and the locale switch is performed by the `tmhDynamicLocale` service provided by the angular-dynamic-locale module. We demonstrated a simple and elegant solution to the locale switch issue, thanks to the efforts of the module author. You can explore this example in the `Example2` folder from the source code for this chapter.

# Other internationalization-related topics

We implemented the code to switch the locale, but we also introduced a potential issue. The currency filter now matches the selected locale, but the prices do not change when we switch the locale. It is not unheard of that some companies have maintained the same price for their products across currencies such as the U.S. dollar, British pound, and euro, but we still need to take the locale ID into account when working with currencies. A possible solution is to pass the selected locale ID with every web service request using HTTP headers. Another is to use the angular-dynamic-locale module support to store the locale ID as a session cookie with the AngularJS `$cookieStore` service from the `ngCookies` module. Both approaches involve further server-side processing, such as the conversion of every currency value to and from a base currency depending on the locale ID associated with the web service request.

Both AngularJS and the module discussed in this section can't resolve the problem of the user interface text changing depending on the current locale ID. Thanks to the efforts of the open source community, there are libraries available, such as angular-translate at `http://angular-translate.github.io/` and angular-gettext at `http://angular-gettext.rocketeer.be/`, that provide user interface translation functionality. As the subject of user interface translation is vast and exceeds the scope of this book, we will stop here, with the mention of two notable libraries that will help you further along.

# Using AngularJS animations

AngularJS 1.2 introduced a new module, `ngAnimate`, that brings animation support for a series of built-in directives such as `ngRepeat`, `ngSwitch`, `ngView`, and `ngClass`, and to custom directives through the `$animate` service. The animation functionality adds specific CSS classes to the HTML elements associated with a directive. For example, the `ngView` directive will add an `ng-enter` class while a new view is being loaded and an `ng-leave` class while an existing view is being unloaded. Using CSS3 transitions or animations, we can implement styles that target these classes and provide special effects to AngularJS. Animations implemented using JavaScript are also supported for older browsers that do not have CSS3 transitions and animations, such as Internet Explorer 8 and 9. Due to a significant difference in performance between the CSS3 and JavaScript implementations, we will only discuss CSS3-based animations in this section.

To show the `ngAnimate` module functionality, we will use a CSS library called Animate.css that implements different types of animations. This library is not related to AngularJS and is a great example of how AngularJS animations integrate seamlessly with CSS3. Animate.css uses CSS3 animations and provides effects such as fading, sliding, bouncing, and flipping, and it is a good base to explore how keyframe animations are built and how to create your own. We will implement the `ng-enter` animation for the `ngView` directive so that when we open the start page of the main sample application or switch to a new view, the HTML will slide in from the right of the page. First, we need to add the NuGet packages for the `ngAnimate` module and the Animate.css library:

```
Install-Package AngularJS.Animate -Version 1.2.15
Install-Package animate.css
```

After the files from these two packages are included in the script and CSS bundles, the `ngAnimate` module needs to be added as a dependency to our application module. The only thing left to do then is define a CSS style that targets the `ngView` directive and the `ng-enter` animation hook in `app.css`, as shown in the following code:

```css
div[data-ng-view] .ng-enter {
    -webkit-animation: slideInRight 1s;
    -moz-animation: slideInRight 1s;
    -o-animation: slideInRight 1s;
    animation: slideInRight 1s;
}
```

Note that the CSS3 vendor prefixes are used to ensure backward compatibility for older versions of Google Chrome, Safari, and Mozilla Firefox. Internet Explorer 8 and 9 do not support CSS3 animations and Internet Explorer 10 and higher do not need a vendor prefix, so the `-ms-animation` style was omitted. The `slideInRight` animation is supplied by the Animate.css library, but you can choose other animations as well, as showcased at `http://daneden.github.io/animate.css`. You can explore this example in the `Example3` folder from the source code for this chapter.

You can find more details on AngularJS animations at `http://code.angularjs.org/1.2.15/docs/guide/animations` and on Animate.css integration at `www.divshot.com/blog/tips-and-tricks/angular-1-2-and-animate-css` and `http://odetocode.com/blogs/scott/archive/2014/02/25/easy-animations-for-angularjs-with-animate-css.aspx`.

# Working with remote web services

A common occurrence for JavaScript-based applications is working with data provided by remote web services. This scenario needs to address the same-origin policy enforced by the browser, where scripts running on a page are prevented from accessing DOM elements or other resources that have a URI domain different from the URI domain of the page. A domain is defined by the combination of the URI scheme, hostname, and port number, and the same-origin policy means that a script running on a page hosted at `http://example.com/main` cannot make an XMLHttpRequest call for the data available at `http://anotherexample.com/api/resources`. To overcome this policy, there are two main techniques—JSONP (JSON with padding) and **Cross-origin Resource Sharing (CORS)**—that can be used, and both are supported by AngularJS.

JSONP is a technique where remote data is requested through a `<script>` element that is usually injected dynamically in the page at application runtime. The request will contain a `callback` URI parameter, which will be used in the response in the form of a JavaScript function call that takes the response data as an argument. For a JSONP request, such as `http://example.com/items/1?callback=getItem`, the response will be `getItem({"id": 1, "name": "item1"});`. JSONP requests can only be GET HTTP requests, and they are supported by a wide range of older browsers, down to Internet Explorer 6. This technique requires minimum server-side changes, and you can find more details about it at `http://json-p.org/`.

CORS is a technique that extends the XMLHttpRequest API and sends an additional HTTP header called Origin with any request to the remote server. This header is set to the request domain, for example, `http://example.com/main`. For each request, the returned response should have a header called Access-Control-Allow-Origin, which should be set to the request domain or to the * value. When this value is set, it means the remote server has acknowledged the CORS request and accepted the request domain.

The browser will also execute an OPTIONS HTTP method first for requests, such as POST or PUT, that have potential side effects in what is known as the preflight of the request.

CORS is based on a W3C specification, `www.w3.org/TR/cors`, and it works with all HTTP methods and is only supported on Internet Explorer 8 and higher. This technique requires more complex server-side changes, but both JSONP and CORS are widely supported by web service frameworks.

To demonstrate these techniques, we will add two new screens for our sample application. One will display a list of company news from a remote web service using JSONP and then CORS, and another one will allow application users to post feedback to a remote web service using CORS.

# Using JSONP

We will start by creating an additional ServiceStack web service project called RentThatBike.WebServices, which is similar to the projects created in *Chapter 3, Creating .NET Web Services for AngularJS*. It has only one unsecured route, which will return a list of NewsItem objects at the address http://localhost:53030/news.

We will add a **News** view to the application, which is accessible from the main menu. The NewsController associated with the view will use the service called newsService to get data from the resource mapped to the news list address. The following is the initial implementation for newsService:

```
myAppModule.factory('newsService', ['$resource', function
($resource) {
  var NewsResource = $resource('http://localhost:53030/news');
  return {
      getNews: function () {
          return NewsResource.query();
      }
  };
}]);
```

When navigating to the **News** page and implicitly executing the NewsResource. query() method, we will see the following error in the JavaScript console of the browser:

**XMLHttpRequest cannot load http://localhost:53030/news. No 'Access-Control-Allow-Origin' header is present on the requested resource. Origin 'http://localhost:61803' is therefore not allowed access.**

AngularJS will attempt to use CORS by default every time it is requesting data from a remote domain, and it will fail because our web services are not yet configured for either JSONP or CORS. We need to change both the AngularJS code and the web services code so JSONP is used as the preferred method first. The RentThatBike. WebServices project needs only one small change to be made in the AppHost. Configure method, which configures ServiceStack for JSONP support, as shown in the following code:

```
SetConfig(new EndpointHostConfig
{
  AllowJsonpRequests = true
});
```

On the client side, the `newsService` definition needs to be changed to the following code:

```
myAppModule.factory('newsService', ['$resource', function
($resource) {
  var NewsResource = $resource('http://localhost:53030/news',
{},
    {
        queryWithJSONP: {
            method: 'JSONP',
            params: {
                callback: 'JSON_CALLBACK'
            },
        isArray: true
        }
    });
  return {
    getNews: function () {
        return NewsResource.queryWithJSONP();
    }
  };
}]);
```

Note that the new `queryWithJSONP` method has been used instead of the usual `query` method. This new method defines an AngularJS-specific `callback` parameter, used internally to generate the remote data request. When the solution is executed, the news items are loaded correctly on the **News** page. If you inspect the request and response details, you will see that the request is sent as `http://localhost:53030/news?callback=angular.callbacks._0`, for which the following response is returned:

```
angular.callbacks._0([
{"created": "2014-06-01T22:05:03.3390875Z",
"title": "Our sales are up",
"content": "Due to unprecedented good weather our sales are up 10%
compared to the same period last year."},
   ...
])
```

AngularJS will dynamically generate the request URL so it can create multiple requests for the same resource simultaneously. You can explore this example in the `Example4` folder from the source code for this chapter.

Before running the example, you need to set up multiple startup projects for the `RentThatBike_With_Nodejs` or `RentThatBike` solution in Visual Studio. If you right-click on the solution node in **Solution Explorer**, there is a **Set StartUp Projects...** menu item that will allow the selection of both `RentThatBike.WebServices` and `RentThatBike.Web` as solution startup projects.

 All of the source code changes made so far in this chapter were removed in the current and following examples to reduce the complexity of the code base.

# Using CORS

CORS is viewed as the modern replacement for JSONP, and it is supported in the ServiceStack web framework with a simple and flexible configuration. To enable CORS support in our web services project, we just need to add the following line of code in `AppHost.Configure`:

```
Plugins.Add(new CorsFeature());
```

As AngularJS will use CORS for any request with a URI domain that is different from the application domain, we don't need to make any special changes in the JavaScript code. We just need to change the `newsService.getNews()` method to use the original `query` method, and the application should load the news list correctly, just like in the previous example.

The `CorsFeature` plugin default constructor used previously will allow CORS requests from any domain using any HTTP method by default. We can easily change it so it allows only GET requests from our specific AngularJS application URI domain with this configuration, as shown in the following code:

```
Plugins.Add(new CorsFeature(new[] { "http://localhost:61803" },
allowedMethods: "GET"));
```

This allows us to tighten the security of the web services at a global level and use a whitelist approach to filter incoming requests.

 You can find more details on CORS configuration options in ServiceStack from an answer posted by the framework author at `http://stackoverflow.com/a/8215777/523296`.

We can now implement the post feedback feature that relies on the CORS technique for non-GET requests, where we allow anyone to send company feedback from the main sample application or through a web service client. We will create a new **Send feedback** menu item and a matching view, which will post feedback with a title and description to the web services hosted by the `RentThatBike.WebServices` project, as shown in the following screenshot:

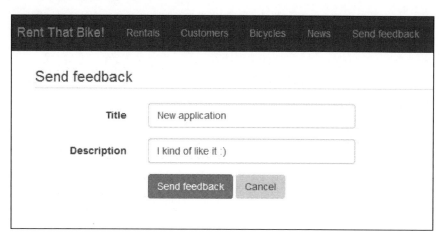

The view will use a `FeedbackController` component very similar to `BicycleController`, with the difference that it will display an alert with the feedback ID once submitted to demonstrate that the server-side code works as expected. The following `feedbacksService` definition is simple and concise and does not have anything special to enable CORS support:

```
myAppModule.factory('feedbacksService', ['$resource', function
($resource) {
  var FeedbackResource =
$resource('http://localhost:53030/feedbacks');
  return {
      createFeedback: function () {
          return new FeedbackResource({});
      },
      addFeedback: function (feedback) {
          return feedback.$save();
      }
  };
}]);
```

On the server side, we need to perform some light, additional configuration to allow OPTIONS HTTP preflight requests because the send feedback request is a POST request. First, we need to make sure ServiceStack does not fully process the OPTIONS requests by adding the following code in `AppHost.Configure`:

```
PreRequestFilters.Add((httpReq, httpRes) =>
  {
      if (httpReq.HttpMethod == "OPTIONS")
          httpRes.EndRequest();
  });
```

The convenient `PreRequestFilters` collection allows us to register custom request filters in a way that resembles the ASP.NET MVC global filter registration. The filter we used will check for OPTIONS requests and end them before being processed by the ServiceStack pipeline, which in effect will return a response with empty data as soon as possible.

The second change we need to make is in the feedback request route definition so it accepts the OPTIONS HTTP verb as shown in the following code:

```
[Route("/feedbacks", "POST, OPTIONS")]
public class Feedback: IReturn<Feedback>
{
  public int Id { get; set; }
  public string Title { get; set; }
  public string Description { get; set; }
}
```

 ServiceStack Version 4 does not require this step as all OPTIONS requests are allowed on it by default.

The `FeedbacksService` class contains the required web service method that just sets the `Id` property to a random value as shown in the following code:

```
public Feedback Post(Feedback request)
{
  request.Id = new Random().Next();
  return request;
}
```

This contrived example showcases how few changes we need to make for full CORS support in the server-side code when using a modern web service framework such as ServiceStack. As AngularJS supports CORS by default, with no changes required, this technique should be an essential tool when designing web services for clients that are not compliant with the same-origin policy.

You can explore the code for this section in the `Example5` folder from the source code for this chapter.

# Template caching

The last section of the chapter is about further optimizations around the load time of our main sample application. A good strategy to load web application resources faster is to minimize the number of required requests. We already explored bundling and minification with ASP.NET MVC in *Chapter 4, Creating an AngularJS, ASP. NET MVC, ServiceStack Application*, and this will ensure that the JavaScript and CSS files are loaded efficiently. However, if we inspect the requests executed by our application, we'll notice that for every AngularJS view that we navigate to, there is an initial request that asks for its matching HTML file. When we load the start page of the application, we will see the request for the `default.html` file from `scripts/app/views/` that contains the HTML for the first view. If we navigate to a different view and back again, we will notice that this file is not requested anymore unless we refresh the page in the browser.

AngularJS uses a `$templateCache` service behind the scenes to cache any HTML template that is requested by `ngInclude`, `ngView`, or other directives. It uses the name of the HTML file as the cache ID so any subsequent requests for the same filename will retrieve the file contents from the cache. This default behavior may cause a noticeable delay between the moment when the page elements start to become visible in the browser and the moment when the page is fully loaded. Connections with low latency or views that have significant HTML content are usually the main cause for this delay. Fortunately, the `$templateCache` service allows the preloading of HTML templates, so when the application page elements become visible, all of the application views are already loaded and available for immediate rendering. To preload an HTML template, we use a `script` tag with a special type that contains the HTML template as shown in the following code:

```
<script type="text/ng-template" id="newContent.html">
  <h1>New content available now</h1>
  <p>There is some new content available.</p>
</script>
```

You can also reference the `$templateCache` service in the `run` section of the application module and preload the HTML template using the following code:

```
myAppModule.run(['$templateCache', function($templateCache) {
    $templateCache.put('newContent.html', '<h1>New content available
now</h1><p>There is some new content available.</p>');
}]);
```

As we are using ASP.NET MVC as the gateway to all application resources, we could preload the HTML templates using a similar technique to share data between server and client, which was explored in *Chapter 4, Creating an AngularJS, ASP.NET MVC, ServiceStack Application*. We will embed the HTML files from the `views` folder at `scripts/app/` within the `script` tags with the `id` set to the relative path of the contained HTML file. For example, for the `default.html` file from the `target` folder, we will use the element tag `<script type="text/ng-template" id="scripts/app/views/default.html">`. The `id` value matches the one used in `app.js` for `$routeProvider` based route definitions so the `ngView` directive will load the view directly from the `$templateCache` service rather than creating an initial HTTP request for it. The only thing left to do is to implement the logic that will extract the content of the HTML files and inject it into the start page of the application. We will store the content in a `ViewBag` property in the `HomeController.Index` controller action as shown in the following code:

```
var scriptsFolderPath = Server.MapPath("~/scripts/app/views");
var scriptsDirectoryInfo = new DirectoryInfo(scriptsFolderPath);
FileInfo[] scriptFileInfos = scriptsDirectoryInfo.GetFiles();
var scriptsStringBuilder = new StringBuilder();
scriptFileInfos.ForEach(scriptFileInfo =>
{
    scriptsStringBuilder.AppendFormat(@"<script type=""text/ng-
template"" id=""scripts/app/views/{0}"">",
        scriptFileInfo.Name);
    scriptsStringBuilder.AppendLine();
    scriptsStringBuilder.Append(System.IO.File.ReadAllText(scriptF
ileInfo.FullName));
    scriptsStringBuilder.AppendLine();
    scriptsStringBuilder.Append("</script>");
    scriptsStringBuilder.AppendLine();
});
ViewBag.AppPartials = scriptsStringBuilder.ToString();
```

Each `script` element is formatted so it can fit nicely on the page and be visually inspected easily. The HTML content needs to be loaded under the element that has the `ngApp` directive, and it is inserted as the last element of the `head` section in the `_Layout.cshtml` file, as shown in the following code:

```
@Html.Raw(ViewBag.AppPartials)
```

When the application is executed, no further HTML file requests will be made and all of the views will load their content directly from the cache.

You can explore these changes in the `Example6` folder from the source code for this chapter. You will notice that all of the JavaScript bundles apart from `browser-support` were merged into a single `common-scripts` bundle and that the bundles are now minified. The application will start with a grand total of four requests, and no other resources apart from web service requests should be made from that point on.

 You can also use the `$templateCache` service to override HTML templates that were loaded by third-party directives and provide your own templates instead.

# Summary

This chapter introduced us to advanced topics, starting with internationalization and localization. We explored the AngularJS built-in support together with a module that allows easy switching between different locales, and we discussed other libraries that will help with managing different translations for the user interface. We then discussed the animation support introduced in AngularJS 1.2 and used simple integration with an animations library to add special effects to our sample application. We also explored working with remote web services and two established techniques that work well with AngularJS. The chapter concluded with a solution to preload HTML templates using ASP.NET MVC, paving the way to a fast and responsive web application.

# Index

## E

ECMAScript 5  27
end-to-end tests, AngularJS application
  implementing  146
  Protractor, configuring  147, 148
  Protractor, installing  146
  Protractor tests, writing  148-150
Entity Framework  125
example, AngularJS  13-16
expect function  142
explicit dependency injection  28

## F

FeedbackController component  174
filters
  overview  40-42
Fluent Assertions
  URL  155
FluentValidation library
  about  88
  URL, for supported validations  88

## G

getBicycles() method  67
getBicycleTypes() method  67
GetPlayers class  84
GET web service methods
  BicyleRepository property  92
  implementing  92
Google Chrome Windows Resizer extension
  URL  55

## H

HTML5 validation support  160
HTML5 validation tool
  URL  161
Hypermedia as the Engine of Application
    State (HATEOAS)  77

## I

i18n. *See* internationalization
IHttpRequest  86
IHttpResponse  86

Immediately-invoked Function
    Expression (IIFE)  24
implicit dependency injection  28
inject function  143
injector  28
interceptor  122
internationalization
  about  164
  issues  164
Internet Explorer 8 support  161, 162
Internet Explorer 9 support  161
Internet Information Services Server
    Express (IIS Express)  128
IService marker interface  83

## J

Jasmine
  URL  142
  used, for creating AngularJS unit tests  141
Jasmine essentials  142
Java Development Kit (JDK)
  about  146
  URL  146
JavaScript design patterns
  online resource  26
JavaScript libraries
  AngularJS, integrating with  58
JavaScript patterns, AngularJS application
  about  24
  Immediately-invoked Function
      Expression (IIFE)  24
  revealing module pattern  25, 26
jqLite  60
jQuery example, AngularJS  10-12
JSONP (JSON with padding)
  about  78, 170
  URL  170
  using  171, 172

## K

Karma
  about  134, 139
  configuring  140, 141
  installing  139, 140

## Thank you for buying
# Learning AngularJS for .NET Developers

# About Packt Publishing

Packt, pronounced 'packed', published its first book "*Mastering phpMyAdmin for Effective MySQL Management*" in April 2004 and subsequently continued to specialize in publishing highly focused books on specific technologies and solutions.

Our books and publications share the experiences of your fellow IT professionals in adapting and customizing today's systems, applications, and frameworks. Our solution based books give you the knowledge and power to customize the software and technologies you're using to get the job done. Packt books are more specific and less general than the IT books you have seen in the past. Our unique business model allows us to bring you more focused information, giving you more of what you need to know, and less of what you don't.

Packt is a modern, yet unique publishing company, which focuses on producing quality, cutting-edge books for communities of developers, administrators, and newbies alike. For more information, please visit our website: www.packtpub.com.

# About Packt Open Source

In 2010, Packt launched two new brands, Packt Open Source and Packt Enterprise, in order to continue its focus on specialization. This book is part of the Packt Open Source brand, home to books published on software built around Open Source licenses, and offering information to anybody from advanced developers to budding web designers. The Open Source brand also runs Packt's Open Source Royalty Scheme, by which Packt gives a royalty to each Open Source project about whose software a book is sold.

# Writing for Packt

We welcome all inquiries from people who are interested in authoring. Book proposals should be sent to author@packtpub.com. If your book idea is still at an early stage and you would like to discuss it first before writing a formal book proposal, contact us; one of our commissioning editors will get in touch with you.

We're not just looking for published authors; if you have strong technical skills but no writing experience, our experienced editors can help you develop a writing career, or simply get some additional reward for your expertise.

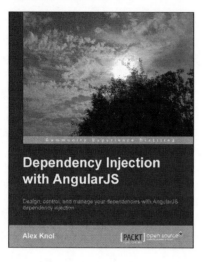

## Dependency Injection with AngularJS

ISBN: 978-1-78216-656-6     Paperback: 78 pages

Design, control, and manage your dependencies with AngularJS dependency injection

1. Understand the concept of dependency injection.

2. Isolate units of code during testing JavaScript using Jasmine.

3. Create reusable components in AngularJS.

## Mastering Web Application Development with AngularJS

ISBN: 978-1-78216-182-0     Paperback: 372 pages

Build single-page web applications using the power of AngularJS

1. Make the most out of AngularJS by understanding the AngularJS philosophy and applying it to real-life development tasks.

2. Effectively structure, write, test, and finally deploy your application.

3. Add security and optimization features to your AngularJS applications.

Please check **www.PacktPub.com** for information on our titles

## AngularJS Directives

ISBN: 978-1-78328-033-9          Paperback: 110 pages

Learn how to craft dynamic directives to fuel your single-page web applications using AngularJS

1. Learn how to build an AngularJS directive.

2. Create extendable modules for plug-and-play usability.

3. Build apps that react in real time to changes in your data model.

## ASP.NET Web API
## Build RESTful web applications and services on the .NET framework

ISBN: 978-1-84968-974-8          Paperback: 224 pages

Master ASP.NET Web API using .NET Framework 4.5 and Visual Studio 2013

1. Clear and concise guide to the ASP.NET Web API with plentiful code examples.

2. Learn about the advanced concepts of the WCF-windows communication foundation.

3. Explore ways to consume Web API services using ASP.NET, ASP.NET MVC, WPF, and Silverlight clients.

Please check **www.PacktPub.com** for information on our titles

Printed in Great Britain
by Amazon